Japanese Bobtail Cats

Japanese Bobtail Cat Owners Manual.

Japanese Bobtail Cats care, personality, grooming, health and feeding all included.

by

Henry Hoverstone

ALL RIGHTS RESERVED. This book contains material protected under International and Federal Copyright Laws and Treaties.

Any unauthorized reprint or use of this material is strictly prohibited. No part of this book may be reproduced or transmitted in any form or by any means, electronic, mechanical or otherwise, including photocopying or recording, or by any information storage and retrieval system without express written permission from the author.

Copyrighted © 2015

Published by: IMB Publishing

Table of Contents

Table of Contents 3

Foreword 7

Acknowledgements 8

Chapter 1: Introduction 9

Chapter 2: The Japanese Bobtail 10

1) What is the Japanese Bobtail? 10
2) Types of the Japanese Bobtail 11
3) What to know before you get one 12
4) Habitat 13
5) The History of the Japanese Bobtail 13
6) Anatomy and Lifespan of the Japanese Bobtail 14

Chapter 3: Physical Characteristics of the Japanese Bobtail 16

1) Head 16
2) Coat 16
3) Color 16

Chapter 4: Personality and Behavior 18

1) Why is it better to have an indoor Cat? 22
2) Your New Japanese Bobtail and Other Cats 24
3) Attention Seeking Disorder in Cats 26
4) Getting Along With Other Pets 30
5) Getting Along With Children 30

Chapter 5: Preparations for the Japanese Bobtail 31

1) Essential supplies for the cat 31

2) Non-essential items 33

3) What to look for in a reputable breeder? 34

4) What breeders are there? 36

5) How to choose the Bobtail 37

6) Older Japanese Bobtails versus kittens 38

7) Where to find the Japanese Bobtail 40

8) Insurance and permits 41

9) Pros and Cons of owning a Japanese Bobtail 42

Chapter 6: Basic Care of the Japanese Bobtail Cat 45

1) Introducing your kitten to your home 45

2) Basic care and routine 50

3) Astuteness 52

4) The Most Charming Cat 53

Chapter 7: Synopsis of the Japanese Bobtail Cat Character 56

Chapter 8: When a Japanese Bobtail is Pregnant 59

1) Reaching Puberty 59

2) Finding the Right Mate 60

3) Important Tips and Guidelines 61

4) Is my Japanese Bobtail in Labor? 62

5) Preparing for Birth 62

6) Danger signs 63

7) Things you must not do during pregnancy 64

Chapter 9: Training the Japanese Bobtail 65

1) Litter box training 65

2) Leash training 68

3) Teaching the cat tricks 70

4) Training a cat to learn new tricks 71

Chapter 10: Grooming the Japanese Bobtail **75**

    1) Benefits of Grooming a Japanese Bobtail cat *76*

    2) Equipment needed for grooming a cat. *78*

    3) Handling and Safety Pointers *78*

    4) Can a Tranquilizer Work? *80*

    5) The Basics of Grooming for Japanese Bobtail Cats *81*

    6) How to Brush the Fur of Your Japanese Bobtail *82*

    7) Trimming the Nails of the Japanese Bobtail cat *83*

    8) Dental Care *85*

    9) Eye Care for the Japanese Bobtail cat *86*

    10) Ear Care of the Japanese Bobtail cat. *86*

    11) Bathing the Japanese Bobtail cat. *87*

Chapter 11: Feeding the Japanese Bobtail **89**

    1) Nutrition. *89*

    2) Water *90*

    3) Proteins *91*

    4) Fats. *92*

    5) Carbohydrates *93*

    6) Vitamins *93*

    7) Minerals *94*

    8) A Word About Milk. *94*

    9) Give your cat a low fat diet *95*

    10) Keep a check on the treats *95*

    11) Say no to crash diets *95*

    12) Keep the activity levels high *96*

    13) Foods you must never give your cat. *98*

Chapter 12: Travelling with your Japanese Bobtail **103**

    1) Travelling by car *103*

2) Travelling by train.. 105

3) Travelling by air.. 105

Chapter 13: Caring for the Japanese Bobtail 107

1) Signs and symptoms of illness.. 107

2) What Causes Stress in These Cats? 110

3) How to Reduce Emotional Stress in Japanese Bobtails 111

4) Examining for specific illnesses 115

5) Medical Disorders 117

6) Spaying and Neutering... 119

7) Vaccinations 124

8) After Vaccination, What's Next? 126

Chapter 14: Finding a Good Vet 128

Chapter 15: The Cost of Owning a Japanese Bobtail.................................. 134

1) Initial Costs... 134

2) Optional Expenses.. 135

3) Ongoing Costs 136

4) Insurance.. 136

Chapter 16: Care for an Aging Cat 138

1) What is aging?.. 138

2) Physiological and Behavioural Changes... 138

3) Health Challenges in Old Cats 140

4) What to Do With an Old Japanese Bobtail Cat...................................... 142

5) How to Cope with Your Japanese Bobtail Cat's Death 147

6) Replacing Your Dead Japanese Bobtail Cat 147

Conclusion 149

Foreword

My experience with the Japanese Bobtail cat is rather vast and I am hoping that this book will help you know more about everything you need to understand about this breed. The Japanese Bobtail is a great cat breed that is wonderful and a real pleasure to be around.

All cats are different and the Japanese Bobtail is no exception. This cat is one that is beautiful and handsome and will be a friend for life if you take good care of it.

I feel that this book will provide you with all the information that you could ever require when it comes to understanding how to take care of the Japanese Bobtail cat breed. Read on and you will learn all sorts of amazing facts about this breed as well as how to have a cat like this in your home

Acknowledgements

I never had the chance to deal with animals until my little sister brought home a stray cat.

The Japanese Bobtail cat that she brought home looked rather unusual, with the cat's tail being so different in appearance from what I am normally used to seeing out of a cat. That wasn't the big issue at the start though.

I was a little bit annoyed because of the non-stop "meows" that had been going in and out of the house ever since that Japanese Bobtail was brought into my home. One day, the cat got sick and my sister decided to bring the cat to me. Once I took it to the vet, he explained the problem, what had to be done and what had to be avoided and I finally learned how to take care of the cat the right away. It was a great moment of bonding for my sister and myself.

My biggest thanks for this book go to my sister, as it was her who introduced me to the world of cats. I was never a fan of cats until I learnt from her and her Japanese Bobtail just how amazing these animals could be. I learnt how to be patient and my sincerity paid off when, little by little, the number of cats that I owned increased in numbers.

Not surprisingly, I have developed a strong fascination for the Japanese Bobtail. This is one of the world's most unique cat breeds.

Hereby, I am sharing some insights and thoughts about my experience with taking care of a Japanese Bobtail cat. I have become a true cat lover and I want to share my interest in this amazing breed with you.

Chapter 1: Introduction

Do you own a Japanese Bobtail cat? Do you want to own one? What information do you need before embarking on this journey of owning a cat? Are you a cat owner but you're not sure if the breed you have is a genuine Japanese Bobtail? All these questions and more about this amazing and fascinating cat breed will be discussed in this book.

This type of cat is a very unique and special cat. It has its own interesting physical features and traits that make it different from other breeds.

Of course, you need to be aware of how you can take care of your Japanese Bobtail. You need to see how you can groom the cat, feed it and provide it with the right forms of medical care as needed.

The Japanese Bobtail cat is a very special type of cat. This guide will help you learn everything that you have ever wanted to explore about the cat breed. The purpose of this book is to help you be the best possible caregiver that you could ever be.

The Japanese Bobtail is no ordinary cat – it is a beautiful and friendly cat that all people will love having in their homes. Be sure to take a look at this book in order to get ideas on what you can do with this cat and how this cat will behave in particular.

Chapter 2: The Japanese Bobtail

1) What is the Japanese Bobtail?

The Japanese Bobtail is a cat breed that is known for having a tail that is bobbed in its appearance. This makes the cat's tail look more like a rabbit's tail. This cat is a native of Japan and its surrounding areas and has only in recent times begun to be identified by people in others parts of the world as a viable cat breed.

This cat has a silky coat that is soft in its texture and typically has an undercoat to it. The coat's length can vary by each cat. It is not uncommon to find Japanese Bobtails that have shorter or longer coats than others.

This is a breed that is rather small in size; males can be around 8 to 12 pounds in weight while females are typically 8 pounds in weight at the most.

The eyes are oval-shaped and will typically feature amber, aqua, green, hazel or orange eyes depending on the cat you find. The rest of the head is triangular in shape. The ears are upright and pointed at right angles. The nose has a slight dip to it while the cheekbones are easily visible.

In addition, the body has a rectangular look to it. The rear legs are slightly longer than the front legs but the difference between the two will vary by each individual cat.

The paws are oval-shaped and rather small in size. The cat also has five toes on its front paws and four on its back paws.

One interesting aspect of the Japanese Bobtail cat is that it is a breed that is known to get along quite well with many others. The cat is known to get along with other cats and even with most dogs. The Japanese Bobtail has been especially heralded for being a breed that does very well with children.

The Japanese Bobtail has especially become popular for being much smarter than many other cats. The Bobtail is smart enough to be able to know its name and to respond to it when it is called.

It is also rather active and enjoys getting plenty of exercise. Naturally, you will have to be rather careful if you are going to have such a cat in the house as the Japanese Bobtail is not going to feel happy if it is left alone in a home for a while. You can always get toys for the cat but remember that it does extremely well with many other cats or dogs in the home.

2) Types of the Japanese Bobtail

The Japanese Bobtail is not necessarily a cat that is bred with many others. As a result, it is a cat that is typically going to be pure on its own.

Needless to say, not much is known about what types of cats the Japanese Bobtail came from. This will be discussed in a little more detail when talking about the history of the breed.

A big aspect of the cat is that it will have many forms based primarily on its coat. Many Japanese Bobtails will have their own different patterns to them.

For instance, a tortoise shell cat will have a coat that features two colors other than white and are scattered around the top of the cat's body. This makes it look like a tortoise shell, hence the name.

The tabby look is another style that the Japanese Bobtail may be found in. This look has stripes, dots and other patterns plus an M-shaped mark on its forehead.

Some of these cats may also be calico cats. This type of cat will feature a mostly white body with patches that come from two other colors.

Still, many of these cats are also found with solid colors. These include lighter colors for the most part but some brown Japanese Bobtails may be found as well.

3) What to know before you get one

There are many things to ask before getting a Japanese Bobtail. Ask yourself; does it suit your demands as a person? Does it also suit your way of life, or rather; does it accentuate your personality? Sometimes, it may be a present for your kids and the decision may not entirely lie on you on which to pick. However, a little guidance does not harm anyone at all. Pointing out the crucial features is a big point to keep an eye out for.

First and foremost, understand the temperament of this particular cat. Is this the first cat you are looking to buy? If not, how well do you relate to them? For most pet keepers, there is a mutual understanding that has to exist for a smooth co-existence. Due to the intelligence that the Japanese Bobtail exhibits, it demands more from its owner. It can easily integrate with people of all kinds, whether old or young.

In addition, you need to understand that this cat is an attention seeker. Sometimes, it may tend to be "annoying" because of how it acts around other pets for those with multiple pets at home. It may also be bothersome like this because of how verbal it can be. This has led to some viewing it as an alpha cat.

Another important concept to keep in mind is that this cat tends to be independent and some individuals who are looking for a lap or cuddle pet are in for a disappointment. While the Japanese Bobtail likes to cuddle with people, it is not necessarily one that likes to be held for too long or is going to be a lap cat for a while.

Chapter 2: The Japanese Bobtail

Check on the condition of the cat before you decide to adopt one into your family. Japanese Bobtails are known to be healthier than many other breeds on average but it helps to talk with a breeder or another party that you might be looking to get the cat from to see if there have been any health issues in that cat's life or within that cat's family tree.

4) Habitat

The Japanese Bobtail is a real charmer but it is also a cat that needs to be observed based on its proper environment. It needs to be in a positive environment that it will be comfortable with if it is going to live long.

The Japanese Bobtail cat can very easily adapt to life in a family home with children, as it is very playful and interactive. It typically fits in better with older children as they might be startled by some sudden or loud actions or behaviors that some smaller children might engage in. However, the cat will not have much of a problem with other pets in the home. It can even get along with dogs quite well. In addition, you may also need more provisions to make it more comfortable such as toys, a scratching post, or even an occasional outdoor play. These can allow for more than enough stimulation that the cat will need for its health. This will be discussed in a later section of this book.

5) The History of the Japanese Bobtail

The Japanese Bobtail has been around since at least the sixth century in Japan. Very little is known about how the cat breed was taken care of in its native country; what is known is that various artifacts in the Niko and Gotokuji Temples in Japan have paintings and woodcuts of the Japanese Bobtail.

The breed is considered to be natural in that its development was never adjusted by any person. The most notable development in the history of the Japanese Bobtail came in 1602 when the Japanese government declared that cats should be set free as a means of capturing and killing rodents who were trying to hurt the silk worms in that country.

Eventually, it became illegal to buy or sell cats. These cats could only be held by farmers who were responsible for producing silk; all other cats lived on the streets. The Japanese Bobtail was the most prevalent of all these cats.

Over time, the Japanese Bobtail became revered as a symbol of luck. The tricolored ones were considered to be the luckiest. This is because a majority of tricolored Bobtails around Japan were female. They were able to produce more appealing Bobtails. In addition, the Maneki Neko statue that features a cat with a raised paw became a symbol of good luck to people all around Japan and can be found in many Japanese shops to this day.

It would not be until 1968 when the Japanese Bobtail was imported into the West. Elizabeth Freret brought the breed over to the United States in that year.

In 1976, the Cat Fanciers' Association officially recognized the shorthair Japanese Bobtail. It would not be until 1993 when the longhaired form of the breed was recognized by the CFA.

Many around the United States and Europe are breeding the cat. Still, it is a rather rare breed.

6) Anatomy and Lifespan of the Japanese Bobtail

You might hear that a cat has nine lives and this is certainly the case for the Japanese Bobtail but its lifespan is not stipulated by any set value. It can live a long, healthy life if you take care of it well. It's important to keep the cat in a clean environment, as this will encourage and even motivate the cat to continue being playful.

A Japanese Bobtail may live for about 10 to 15 years on average if it is kept healthy. You need to ensure that it gets more than

Chapter 2: The Japanese Bobtail

enough exercise and plenty of nutritional support in order to keep it healthy and living for as long as possible.

It's important to keep the cat in a clean environment as this will encourage and even motivate the cat to continue being playful.

This breed is also rather healthy for the most part. It is not known to have any genetic health issues. However, some of these cats may develop obesity. This may be the case if a cat's diet is not controlled as well as it is supposed to be. There are many other health considerations to explore but these will be covered a little later on in this guide.

The cat's anatomy, apart from the tail, is around the same as that of many other cats. It is not going to develop any issues with its organs or other key body parts provided that you take good care of that cat.

Chapter 3: Physical Characteristics of the Japanese Bobtail

The Japanese Bobtail is very different from other cat breeds when compared with so many others. This is thanks to more than just the unique ears that this cat breed has. Many of these characteristics are based on the standards that were provided by the Cat Fanciers' Association.

1) Head

The Japanese Bobtail has a head that is triangle-shaped. The ears are upright and at right angles against each other.

The eyes are also oval-shaped. They may be found in blue, amber, orange, hazel or green colors among many others.

The cheekbones around the head are also rather easy to notice. They are far more defined than they are in other breeds.

2) Coat

A cat's fur is more than a beautiful style. It is also a source of insulation. The Japanese Bobtail can come with short or long hair. Either way, the coat will be silky and smooth. In addition, while a Japanese Bobtail can have long hair, it is only in a semi-long length, thus making it a little easier to manage. This breed also has a slight undercoat.

3) Color

The Japanese Bobtail can come in many colors. It typically comes in a white, cream, brown or a silver color for the most part.

Chapter 3: Physical Characteristics of the Japanese Bobtail

Some of these cats have a few stripes, spots or points. Tortoise shell and calico Japanese Bobtail cats have been reported in many cases.

The cat will typically have a pink nose and paw pads. Some shadowy parts may be found on some younger cats in this breed.

Chapter 4: Personality and Behavior

The Japanese Bobtail's personality is as striking as its appearance, surpassing many other breeds when it comes to playfulness and affection. The Japanese Bobtail is an intelligent, adorable cat that is especially active. It will continue to stay athletic and strong well into old age.

Needless to say, more research is needed to determine the exact points of a Japanese Bobtail's behavior. One thing that is for certain is that it is a breed that is known to be very happy and is very comfortable around most people and other animals; this is all according to what many Japanese Bobtail owners have reported over the years.

It is very friendly to others and can particularly fit in with other pets in the home and with older children. It especially enjoys toys that allow the cat to recreate hunting activities. That is, the cat will go after items and pounce on them, possibly biting them.

This cat is especially one that will be active at all times of the day. It will enjoy getting plenty of attention and is willing to be active at night. However, it will also enjoy a bit of time to relax in one's lap at night. It is known to be rather affectionate without being overly needy.

A bored Japanese Bobtail can cause a lot of mischief, thus it's important not to leave the cat alone for many hours. It's affectionate and always ready to help and participate in all of your activities. When it wants to play, the Japanese Bobtail can be very persistent and can be destructive just to get the desired attention. The cat is also known for being rather verbal.

Their intelligence enables them to devise ways of opening doors, cabinets and drawers. They have a tendency of concealing themselves in surprising places including closets or even in the cloth basket, which for them is play. A happy Japanese Bobtail

Chapter 4: Personality and Behavior

will roll over on its back with its feet kneading joyfully in the air, accompanied by an extremely loud purr.

The Japanese Bobtail may be interpreted as a lap cat as well. It is small enough to lie down on your lap and will be patient enough to be with you for a while. It will prefer to stay close to you or at least remaining in the room with you. In addition, the Japanese Bobtail loves to snuggle but is willing to get off your lap every once in a while.

The Japanese Bobtail is one breed that loves to be verbal. It can be very vocal and can carry out an animated conversation for the longest time. Its meows are rather varied in terms of their tones.

Japanese Bobtail cats are capable of living in outdoor and indoor situations but they are more comfortable with indoor spaces for the most part. It is comfortable in a majority of conditions but it is best to keep such a cat indoors in a space where the climate is under control.

Even if you do take your Japanese Bobtail outside on occasion, you must make sure that you are around it all the time, as these cats tend to feel a sense of despair when they are alone. However, you might want to watch out when trying to get a leash. Not all Japanese Bobtails are totally comfortable with leashes.

While it is true that this cat is best when staying indoors, there are several reasons why people think that keeping a cat indoors is unfair. Some of the most common myths associated with keeping a cat indoors are:

A lack of exercise can lead to weight issues. – It is not mandatory for a cat to go outdoors to get the exercise that it requires. Especially with a breed like the Japanese Bobtail, it is very easy to prompt them to stay active even indoors. All you need to do is place a cat tree that he/she can climb. Cats also love to sharpen their claws on these cat trees. Japanese Bobtail cats are naturally playful and enjoy hunting games while indoors.

Chapter 4: Personality and Behavior

This means that you can give them toy mice and other pet toys to play with. Even a spool of thread or a paper box can become a great play tool for your pet. The most important thing with an indoor cat is the environment that it lives in. If you can make your home comfortable for the cat to run around and play in, you need not worry about taking him/her outdoors for some exercise.

It is not possible to domesticate a cat to stay indoors. – This is not true, especially with the Japanese Bobtail cat. This breed opts to stay indoors. As for the sunshine and natural environment required by them, they will just enjoy these sights and sounds from a windowsill. They don't always have to go outdoors.

The pet might urinate and dirty the house up. – Cats, as a species, are very easy to toilet train. All you need to do is teach them to use the litter box. With an intelligent cat like the Japanese Bobtail, there is no need to worry about getting the cat toilet trained. One thing that most cat owners observe is that after sometime, the cat urinates outside the box. This typically occurs right next to the box and is not often going to occur in random spots around one's home.

This is only an indication that the litter box is too dirty. It is the cat's way of telling its owner that it is time to have the litter box cleaned up. Most owners think that this behavior is an indication that the cat needs to go outside. Sometimes, it could be an indication that your cat may have some medical requirements. If your cat continues to litter outside the box even after you have cleaned it then make sure you consult a veterinarian.

The cat might scratch and ruin the furniture. – It is true that cats love to keep their claws sharp. So, it is natural for them to scratch hard surfaces as a mechanism to trim and sharpen their claws. If your cat is not trained, then you can expect your furniture to be ruined in just a few days. The solution to this does not come from trimming the nails of your cat. The behavior will persist. The best thing to do would be to provide your cat with a cat tree. In case your cat continues to damage other surfaces in spite of providing it with a tree, you must observe the types of surfaces that he/she likes to sharpen his/her nails on.

All you need to do is cover the cat tree with that material. Each cat has its own preference when it comes to the material that it chooses to scratch. In order to train your cat to use only the cat tree, you may also spray scents like catnip in order to attract the cat to the tree.

It is unhygienic to have a cat at home. – Cats usually tend to walk on high surfaces like kitchen cabinets and shelves. In case you do not find this comfortable or hygienic, you can train the cat to only occupy certain spaces. It is also possible to train your cat to stay away from the kitchen.

In any case, cats are extremely clean creatures. They are constantly bathing or cleaning themselves. Another thing with an indoor cat, the Japanese Bobtail for example, is that the amount of contaminants that it brings in is a lot less than what an outdoor cat might bring in.

Cats infect pregnant women. – One very common reason for most people to keep cats outdoors is the presence of a pregnant woman in the household. Many believe that women who are pregnant can contract a disease called Toxoplasmosis if they come into contact with cat feces by accident.

Unknown to many, this disease is most often caused by the consumption of uncooked meat. However, in order to be safe, pregnant women should always wear gloves while cleaning litter boxes. The cat is not a threat to the wellbeing of the pregnant woman and can be allowed to stay indoors without the danger of any infection.

Now that we have busted the myths about indoor cats, you might also want to consider some rather logical reasons to keep your cat indoors. When you have a cat like the Japanese Bobtail that loves to stay indoors, you will never have to really worry about the well being of your cat.

Chapter 4: Personality and Behavior

1) Why is it better to have an indoor Cat?

There are several reasons why a mostly indoor cat like the Japanese Bobtail is a more convenient option to have in your home when compared to other cat breeds. Here are a few things that you might want to consider if you are thinking of choosing an outdoor cat over an indoor cat:

Traffic is one of the biggest reasons to keep a cat indoors. – If you live close to a highway or reside on a street that is relatively busy, you might want to consider a Japanese Bobtail that will spend most of its time indoors. Even the smallest accident can be fatal for your cat or might result in serious injuries.

Cats that roam outdoors are most susceptible to infections from other cats. – Feline Immunodeficiency Virus or Feline Leukemia is quite common in cats that roam outside. These diseases are usually transmitted from one cat to another. Both the diseases mentioned above are fatal for cats. If you allow your cat to roam freely, there are also several possibilities of catfights with other stray cats in the neighborhood.

This leads to injuries and abscesses that make it hard for both the owner and the Japanese Bobtail. Not only do these injuries cause a lot of pain to your pet, they will also cost you several hundreds of dollars to take care of and treat. If your cat has not been properly vaccinated, then it runs the risk of several other diseases that are prevalent in the outdoors.

Parasites are common issues faced by cats. It is very easy for fleas to attack your cat if it is usually strolling freely outdoors. – Some fleas may also carry diseases that are deadly for the cat as well as its owners.

Some ticks also have the potential to paralyze the cat permanently or even kill it if not treated correctly. Fungi like ringworm can also infect your cat. Ringworm can be passed on from the cat to its owner quite easily. Although it is not a deadly disease, ringworm usually recurs in cats and is not easy to treat or get rid of.

If your cat is outdoors often then there are several other dangers that it will encounter. – Domesticated cats are usually not able to defend themselves against animals like dogs, opossums and snakes and will either end up being seriously injured or even die due to these attacks. If your cat ventures into wrong territories by mistake, it becomes vulnerable to these attacks. Cats are also susceptible to attacks from people as well. There are also times when the cat might get near rain or other forms of water. While water doesn't bother them too much, they can be irritated by it after a while.

A cat that is allowed to roam outdoors is more likely to get lost. – They may also be stolen to be used in labs. In many horrifying instances, cats are killed for trade of fur and even as a part of extremist religious practices. So it is best that you either opt for a cat that stays indoors or at least ensure that it has a collar with information to identify it. According to statistics, close to 10% of cats that have been rescued in animal shelters are not reclaimed by their owners.

Skin cancer is also a problem with most cats that go outdoors. – This is regardless of the color of the cat's coat. If you live in a country or a part of the world where skin cancer is highly prevalent then you must consider protecting your cat from exposure to sunlight. Many cat owners neglect the importance of keeping a cat in an enclosure when left outdoors. You must ensure that the enclosure has enough space for the cat to rest in the shade.

You might also face several social problems when you allow your cat to roam outside. – It is possible that your cat litters your neighbor's garden or simply ruins a beautiful flowerbed. In either case, you might find yourself getting in feuds endlessly with your neighbor. It is impossible to locate and control a cat that is used to the outdoors.

Chapter 4: Personality and Behavior

Although there are several myths surrounding the need for cats to be aloof and independent in the outdoors, you can prove them all wrong with your Japanese Bobtail cat. The fact that the cat loves to stay with its owners shows that it is made to be indoors.

If you feel like your cat is getting bored of the indoors, all you have to do is put in a bit of effort to make the environment more interesting. Especially with a highly intelligent cat like the Japanese Bobtail, you must try to include puzzle toys and other stimulating activities in its routine. You must make sure you spend time with your Japanese Bobtail to keep him/her healthy and happy. This is to allow a cat to feel happy and less likely to be bothered in any particular case.

2) Your New Japanese Bobtail and Other Cats

You should have the final say as to whether or not you need just one Japanese Bobtail in the home or more. The Japanese Bobtail will get along with other cats including ones in the same breed. Therefore, you can choose to have more than one if you want but it is also fine if you just get one.

Still, you might want to also watch for what you are doing with your cat. You need to make sure you allow a new Japanese Bobtail to be comfortable with not only its new surroundings but also with any other cats that might be in the same home.

If you already have a resident cat in your home then you can expect your Japanese Bobtail cat to familiarize itself with the other cat. This is because it is easy for the Japanese Bobtail cat to interact with another cat.

However, if it doesn't easily interact or play with the other cat, it is important as well to make sure that your pet does not feel neglected or out of place. In fact, a Japanese Bobtail might be rather assertive and likely to be defensive in the event that it sees that another cat is trying to attack or do something that the original cat is not all that comfortable with. You can take each

Chapter 4: Personality and Behavior

step at a time to make the situation more relaxed for you, the older cat and the new cat in the house.

The first direct interaction should be scheduled over a weekend. – This will make sure that you have all day to spend with the new cat and your resident cat. You can make sure that there are no unpleasant interactions. It is always best to have these interactions during meal times. You can expect some growling and hissing but it will not be entirely aggressive. To make sure that it does not get out of hand, you must place the feeding bowls at opposite ends of the room. Once the feeding is done, separate them instantly.

Cats are territorial by nature. So make sure you establish the boundaries for both cats. – When your new cat is out of the confinement of its bonding room, you might want to make a special corner for him that is not too close to the existing space of your resident cat. Just place the feeding bowl and the cat bed in the designated area with your cat's favorite toys.

The interactions between your cats must be gradual. –You can try the blanket switching technique with cats as well. They will become comfortable with one another when they are accustomed to each other's scent. You must allow them to spend more time with each other slowly. Don't leave them unsupervised until you are assured that they are relaxed in each other's company. Until then, you must never leave them unattended in the same space. This is especially true in the evening.

If you have more than one cat at home, you will notice that one of the resident cats will take the initiative to introduce the new cat to the existing group.

It is common for the cats to not get along immediately. If this is true for your resident cats and the new kitten, make sure you do not punish either of them. Just separate them when they get anxious. You must understand that this behavior is purely instinctive. With regular interactions, the cats will learn to live together peacefully.

Chapter 4: Personality and Behavior

When you see cats fighting amongst themselves, you will not consider it a big deal. This is especially true when you own more than one cat. However, it is wise to be watchful when your pets get into a fight.

You have to ensure that the fight does not turn ugly. This, much like a human brawl, can have serious repercussions. Catfights are mostly attributed to fear, territorial misunderstandings, venting to let off stress, anxiety and more.

There are various kinds of aggression that are seen in cats. These include the following cases:

Sexual aggression – Sexual aggression in animals is quiet a common phenomenon. However, in cats it is not very commonly seen. When two cats get sexually aggressive towards each other, the dominating cat bites the victim cat's nape and there is an attempt to climb on the victim cat.

Territorial aggression – This sort of aggression is also observed quiet often amongst all animals. Much like dolphins, dogs and other animals, cats are also known to mark their territory. Cats urinate to mark their territory. The dominating cat is seen hissing, growling and readying himself to jump on his victim.

Usually, the trespassing cat turns around respectfully and walks away. In some cases, the victim or the trespasser cat will put up a fight and things turn ugly. One interesting thing to note is: the cat that marks its territory need not be the oldest cat or the cat that has lived in the house for the longest period of time.

3) Attention Seeking Disorder in Cats

Cats like the Japanese Bobtail are known to 'meow' nonstop at certain times of the day or night. Their constant howling can become a nuisance for the owner. Before one jumps the gun, and comes to the worst conclusion, it is sensible to sit down and understand what is causing your cat to behave in this particular manner.

Chapter 4: Personality and Behavior

The howling of your cat can be broadly categorized as either crying or meowing. The cause for such behavior can be either emotional or physical pain that the cat is experiencing. Experts have noted that the attention-seeking demeanor of the cats can be further classified as follows.

Mournful howl – Some cats tend to howl in the night like they are calling out for help. This particular howl can make the cat owner cringe with sympathy for the poor creature. This mournful howl is mostly a result of deafness. In some cases, this cry has been identified as the cat's cry for help in its old age. It is also associated with the insanity of an old cat. The reason for this howl need not always be an emotional one.

A certain condition called Feline hyperesthesia is also associated with this behavior. When a cat howls during the night and is found to roll around in the house, you must consider this condition. This condition is commonly called Rippling Skin Disorder. This disorder is considered a stress disorder but the symptoms usually include a set of unrelated issues. The cat tends to become extremely sensitive to touch and the skin begins to show ripples.

The possible causes of this disorder are the excessive presence of unsaturated fatty acids in combination with Vitamin E deficiency, brain infection or trauma, and flea allergies. If the cat is diagnosed with this disorder then it is unlikely that it will be completely cured. So, paying attention to these issues can help you provide greater comfort to the cat and keep tab on its behavioral issue.

Chronic pseudo hunger – Hunger pangs are commonly observed in cats as well. Like human beings, cats also have food cravings, which are unwarranted. Cats tend to develop a lot of liking towards some treats like tuna flakes. This can also turn into an addiction of sorts.

The figure 8 – Cats are known to run around their owner's feet in circles. This is also categorized under attention seeking issues of

Chapter 4: Personality and Behavior

the cat. They are much like kids who need a little bit of extra attention. They also tend to rub themselves against your arm when they need extra attention.

Meow chat – Cats are very vocal. They also like to have conversations with their owners. Some chatty cats tend to prod their owners into lengthy conversations. If the owner refuses to spend enough time with the cat then the cat will tend to suffer from excessive loneliness.

Scratching – Cats scratch; this is common knowledge. Sometimes they overdo it and then the owner may have to be a little concerned. Excessive scratching can cause a cat to bleed from its skin. It has been noted that cats use scratching as a tool to demand for your attention. It is best to take note of this behavior before your beloved pet inflicts physical pain on itself.

Contrary to traditional belief, a cat that stays indoors is known to be healthier and happier. Considering all the threats that you are protecting it from, there is no reason why you should not believe this. Research proves that cats that are allowed to stay indoors also have a longer life than cats that are allowed to roam freely.

However, there are some cat owners who are not particularly fond of keeping the cat indoors. Japanese Bobtail cat owners, however, must be willing to keep them in the house. If you are insistent on having a Japanese Bobtail cat but are uncertain about keeping it indoors then you must ensure that you provide it with a good enclosure.

This is the only way to ensure that your cat gets the benefits of staying outdoors while being protected from the dangers that are prevalent. We will discuss in detail about cat enclosures in the following chapters.

The Japanese Bobtail is the best pet to have because of its loyalty, devotion and affection. It makes a good companion even in times when you're sick. It will be there to nurse you back to health. Its amazing personality is what makes its owners spend more time

Chapter 4: Personality and Behavior

with it. They are affectionate to their owners and can relate well to other humans as well but the full adoration falls on the owner. If you love to stay home, you must definitely opt for a Japanese Bobtail cat. This beauty is extremely active and social. They will actually put in sincere efforts to seek your attention. As a result, Japanese Bobtail cats have the tendency to develop idiosyncrasies that are extremely adorable and quite entertaining.

For instance, if your cat notices that you find it funny when he/she chases a spool of thread, you can expect the cat to do it over and over again. They will also condition their behavior to appeal to the entire family. As long as he has your attention, you can be sure that your cat can entertain you quite gladly.

The Japanese Bobtail cat is also quite adept at finding ways to keep itself entertained when it gets bored. This small-sized kitty is packed with energy and requires constant stimulation to expend that energy. What happens if you simply get bored of its antics? Well, he/she will just voice out his/her dissatisfaction at your lack of attention. These Japanese Bobtail cats are highly vocal cats. They are not, in the slightest bit, noisy or annoying. They are just highly responsive by nature. Their call is not the regular "meow" that you expect from a cat.

The call of a Japanese Bobtail cat is rather shrill and unique. The intensity of their purring and calling will also change with their mood. For instance, if you have just come back from work, your Japanese Bobtail will smother you with affection, purring loudly and following you around the house. The cat does not like it when it is left alone for an extended period of time.

With a cat like this, you will find yourself a true companion. They are very patient creatures that are extremely attached to their owners. They like to be played with, cared for and loved. The most amazing thing about the Japanese Bobtail is that it is a highly understanding cat that is sensitive enough to react to your moods perfectly.

Chapter 4: Personality and Behavior

If you are happy, your Japanese Bobtail will rejoice with you. If you are upset, your Bobtail will curl up close to you and will never leave your side. Overall, this is one of the most compassionate cat breeds that you can ask for. This amazing cat breed has the most entertaining personality in comparison to other breeds. It may also be a challenge to have this cat as a pet due to its short attention span. The Japanese Bobtail desires interaction and play.

4) Getting Along With Other Pets

The Japanese Bobtail is known for being a cat that is able to get along with other animals. It can do fine with many pets and will not pick fights if the pet is relaxed and introduced to these other pets. However, it is important to ensure that the cat is not going to be too irritated around other pets. It is often easy for the Bobtail to want to exhibit its dominance and to become rather assertive. That is, it wants to be the main focus of attention in just about any space that it is in. It's a peculiar point that is interesting for all to explore and think about.

5) Getting Along With Children

The Japanese Bobtail will also get along with children quite well. They are relaxed and will enjoy being with them throughout the day. However, children who are more active or ones who are older will be better suited to such a cat. The Bobtail is known to be relatively active and will not want to relax for too much time. In fact, some cats might not listen to children as they tell them to do certain things. It's an interesting aspect that shows just how such a cat can behave.

In fact, smaller and younger children that might make more noise may not be good for a cat like this. These children might startle the cat too often or even hurt the cat by accident. It is typically best to have this cat around older children who are going to be a little more careful. This is for the safety of the cat and the children in the house alike.

Chapter 5: Preparations for the Japanese Bobtail

Preparing to bring a new member of the family home can be a whirlwind of an experience if you don't have the required information. Here I will list some of the essential and non-essential supplies you may need. A Japanese Bobtail is a very playful cat and it needs lots of attention but as a human being, you may not have much time due to work and other schedules in your life. When you make the decision to buy or adopt a Japanese Bobtail, below are some of the essential supplies you will need.

1) Essential supplies for the cat

Supplies for the cat can be divided into two parts; the essential and non-essential items required.

a. Scratching Post
A scratching post is important, especially for playful cats such as the Bobtail. It is classified as an essential item because it's an important plaything for such a cat to have. A scratching post will save you from torn furniture cushions associated with play with the cat.

b. Litter Box
A litter box is the most important item and each cat owner must have one. A litter box is the relieving point of a cat and it should be strategically located. Later in this guide we will discuss the different approaches that you can take when litter training your cat. Home breaking a cat can be cumbersome, especially when your rag smells of cat urine.

A well-trained cat does not urinate outside of its litter box. So, when this happens and you have determined that it is a behavioral problem, then you can take the following measures:

Chapter 5: Preparations for the Japanese Bobtail

Check the litter box and clean it if you have left it without any plans for appropriate cleaning.

Do not make the cat smell its own urine as a punishment. This is nothing but bullying your pet and such behavior will serve no purpose.

Check if your cat is stressed. Any change in its environment causes stress in them. They react very promptly to new family members, renovation of the house etc.

If you find your cat taking a liking for a particular spot in the house, then place the litter box in that area.

Give your cat some more attention. This may be its way of attracting your attention as it has been missing your company.

c. A Cat Carrier

A cat carrier is described as cat transportation. It's an essential item because it will help you when transporting your new cat home from the pet shop. During trips, it is important that your cat is comfortable to avoid becoming a nuisance. Cat carriers come in different sizes so make sure you consult the pet shop owner to get more perspective on the carrier.

d. Brush and Fine Comb

Grooming your cat is an important part of bonding. A brush and fine toothcomb are essential. It is true that the length of the cat's hair may vary but it is important for you to make sure you at least use a good comb to take care of the cat's hair so it will continue to look as well as possible.

A rubber curry brush will be a great product to have. Meanwhile, a fine comb will remove mats in the hair. You can always brush the cat once a week. The odds of it shedding are not all that great but it helps to brush the coat once a week just to be sure the cat is comfortable.

Chapter 5: Preparations for the Japanese Bobtail

The topic of grooming will be discussed in a little more detail in the next few Chapters.

e. Cat Pillow
Just as you need comfort on a place of rest, buying a cat pillow will be a great investment. This is mainly because a cat pillow will discourage the cat from laying everywhere in the house, leaving balls of hair. The Japanese Bobtail is a playful cat and it requires adequate comfort. It is also important to keep its sleeping environment very clean.

f. Food and Water Dishes
Cats associate a place they are given food as their home. It's essential to have cat dishes as they feel good when offered food. This will help build a relationship of trust that increases on bonding with your cat.

2) Non-essential items

While these items are not necessarily required, they are still strongly recommended with care in mind.

a. Cat Collar
A collar acts as an identification document for a cat. A cat collar should include the cat owner's name, a reachable number and the cat's name. This way, if the cat ever strayed, the owner may be contacted to pick it up with no worries.

b. Shampoos
The Japanese Bobtail is not the most complicated animal to take care of when it comes to washing it. While you might not have much of a need to give such a cat regular baths like what you'd need to do with a cat with much longer hair, it is still important to at least know what you need to do in order to keep your cat's coat healthy and comfortable. Make sure the cat is fully rinsed out and washed as you use a shampoo. Although the coat is short in length, it can still have tangles and other issues that may make it harder for you to get a shampoo to work as needed.

Chapter 5: Preparations for the Japanese Bobtail

c. Toys

The Japanese Bobtail is a playful cat and requires many toys. Recommendations include fake mice, which give them great hunting skills. Cats are social creatures and interact by playing with toys, which is a great way to create a bond with the cat.

All these supplies are essential in one way or the other. After buying all these essentials you can go ahead and buy the Japanese Bobtail cat and create a great environment. But before you do that, here are some pointers on what to look for when purchasing this animal.

3) What to look for in a reputable breeder?

An ideal breeder will follow the required code of ethics that stops him/her selling it to any pet store or to any wholesaler and he/she fulfills all their responsibilities. Whenever you want to buy a Japanese Bobtail, look for a breeder who has health certification to know if there is any genetic disease in any of the cats, loves being around them, and also who raises them in their own house rather than in some pet store or storage room. This is important because of the fact that cats that are raised in an isolated place are fearful and they take more time to socialize with people.

When it comes to a good breeder, many of them have a website of their own, which makes it very difficult for a person who is trying to buy an Japanese Bobtail to decide which one is good and which one is not.

You need to look into the breeder too. It's reputation as a cattery and the hygienic conditions of the facility are important. The bloodline would also be a factor that you would like to consider before buying your Japanese Bobtail.

Then of course, the color and pattern of the fur and the eye color would be something that you might like to have according to your preference. These factors also affect the price of the cat.

Chapter 5: Preparations for the Japanese Bobtail

Normally, Japanese Bobtail cats can cost around $600/£380 due to the rarity of such cats.

Some cats that are not perfect will cost less; a Japanese Bobtail that may not meet all breed standards may be found for $500/£320.

Be very careful when buying a cat like this. Take all things into account when looking for one that you will enjoy having in the home. Do not in any case rush into buying such a cat. The major problem that you may come across involves finding a reliable cattery. It is so difficult these days to distinguish between the unreliable and reliable breeders. There is nothing you can really do that can guarantee that you don't end up buying an unhealthy kitten, but by going about things in the right way you can certainly reduce the chances.

Firstly, do a thorough research on what breed you want to buy, so that you know what is coming. Secondly, check out the facility very meticulously to see if there are any unhygienic conditions or sick animals in the house. Then you need to know what to ask the breeder. Asking the right questions can spare you a lot of trouble. Asking your veterinarian can also be a good idea. He/she can refer you to a reputable breeder that he/she might know himself.

As it has been mentioned earlier, do not show any haste. Be patient. The breed that you are looking for might take a while to be made available to you. The breeders often do not give away kittens unless they are at least twelve to sixteen weeks of age. Kittens can be fun but at the same time they can be a disaster, until they become somewhat adult. So, an adult Japanese Bobtail cat might be exactly what you need. Be sure to compare options when finding a cat that you will be rather comfortable with having in your home and your life.

Chapter 5: Preparations for the Japanese Bobtail

4) What breeders are there?

You might find that there are many good breeders out there that are useful and appropriate for your needs when finding the Japanese Bobtail cat.

Important: Please note that I have not bought cats from these breeders so make sure that you investigate these thoroughly before you buy from them. There are many breeders trading just to make a profit, who do not really care about the well being of the cats. Please be aware of this.

Here are a few good options to think about when you are trying to find a Japanese Bobtail breeder:

In the United States:

Cat-Chi Cats (Washington DC)

http://www.catchicats.com/

Kurisumasu (Portland, Oregon; they have placed such cats in homes all around the world)

http://www.kurisumasu.org/

Janipurr (San Francisco; again, they also work with homes around the world)

http://www.janipurr.com/

Gulfcats (Texas)

http://www.gulfcats.com/

Needless to say, this arrangement of breeders is rather limited due to the overall scarcity of such cats. Still, you should look carefully when finding such cats to have in your life.

Chapter 5: Preparations for the Japanese Bobtail

5) How to choose the Bobtail

It is very important that you know everything about the cat that you are going to buy so that you are sure about buying the right one.

While you might end up thinking that the Japanese Bobtail is like any other cat, you need to see that it is one that can be rather small in size. It can be less than ten pounds in weight in many cases; this is especially the case for females.

Of course, the Japanese Bobtail is different from many other cats that are out there. You can easily tell apart different types of Japanese Bobtail based on their patterns like the tortoise shell patterns, lynx rings or smoke face prints that they have. You can easily find different types of cats based on these markings.

In addition, you may notice that these cats are rather agile. They do not like to sit around much. They like heights and have average vertical leaps of five feet. Often, they will be spotted perched high.

You may also feel heavily appreciated by such cats, as they are very friendly. They build association with their owner very quickly.

One noticeable feature of these cats is that they can have coats that are varying in length. You might find some shorter coats but there are plenty out there who have semi-long coats as well.

You should still be careful when looking for such a cat. You must talk with a breeder about any particular health issues that one cat's line has experienced. While it is true that such cats are healthier than many others that are out there, you still need to be rather careful when finding such a cat. Always make sure you look into the medical history of any line that you want to adopt from; the lines might be shorter than what they are for many other cat breeds but it's always a good idea to take a careful look at what to expect out of such a cat.

Chapter 5: Preparations for the Japanese Bobtail

Don't forget that the appearance of the tail can make a difference. The amazing part of the bobbed tail is that no two Japanese Bobtails are truly alike in terms of how their tails are built.

6) Older Japanese Bobtails versus kittens

Adult cats are very different from kittens. They will take longer to get used to the household and the people living there. Whether you have rescued or adopted an older cat, there are simple tips and tricks that will help you make the cat feel comfortable. Remember that an adult cat comes with several past experiences.

Its behavior will depend entirely on the kind of interactions that he/she has had with people in the past. You can do a little background check and make necessary adjustments in your lifestyle to accommodate an adult cat. This is especially critical if you have a Japanese Bobtail to deal with.

You should ask your breeder or the owner of the pet rescue centre all the details of your cat's history. – There may be specific toys that the cat is fond of. There may also be special scents or fragrances that the cat might require to feel comfortable. It is also important to know if your cat pet-to-be has had an abusive history. If yes, you must understand completely the things that might make the cat anxious or uncomfortable.

You can keep the adult cat in a cat carrier for a few days. – In case there is a specific bonding room for the new cat, make sure

Chapter 5: Preparations for the Japanese Bobtail

you leave the carrier there. This can become your cat's permanent hideout and also zone of comfort.

The litter box, food and water must be introduced to the new adult cat. – Place them all in the bonding room or the confinement room that the cat is in.

When your cat is ready, you can take it to new parts of your home. – It is absolutely mandatory that you familiarize the cat with all areas of your home. For an indoor cat like this one, being able to look for resting spots and hiding spots becomes possible only when he is comfortable with all the space available.

With an adult cat, conditioning becomes necessary. – The responsibility is on you to make sure that the cat spends ample time around you. You must make time to play with the cat, talk to him/her and just be around him/her. A Japanese Bobtail cat requires more attention than other cats and you must try as hard as you can to keep it happy. Only when the cat is sure of you as the right companion will it open up and be friendly.

Make sure you keep an eye on your new cat. – If it does not eat properly or use the litter box, you might have to seek some help from an expert. Another common problem with adult cats is the development of skin problems. These are all signs of discomfort and unhappiness in the cat.

With a Japanese Bobtail cat, it is easier to overcome these special requirements. This is why it is considered the ideal pet for people who need constant companionship.

Older Japanese Bobtails are more mature and understand easily when it comes to litter training and learning new tricks. The more mature Japanese Bobtail is able to understand the environment better and requires little attention.

Kittens require a lot of attention and care at this age while still adapting to the home environment. New environments easily frighten them and in the next chapter we will discuss the

Chapter 5: Preparations for the Japanese Bobtail

introduction of the cat in the home. Adult cats can attack the new baby cat so it's important for the owner to introduce this new pet without making it look like a competition.

Kittens need a lot of warmth as they grow; therefore, you will need to buy a heater to keep the room warm for the cat. The standards that have to be used for the grooming of the adult and kitten are the same; light brushing once or twice a week even if the cat is not going to shed all that much. Kittens are generally playful and will require tons of toys to keep them busy all the time. Adult Japanese Bobtails are very social and interactive as well.

The choice between an adult and a kitten are dependent on time. If you have time, you can choose to buy a kitten and enjoy the journey as a healthy Bobtail could live for at least twelve years if you are good to it. An adult Japanese Bobtail cat is not time consuming and may be a good choice for busy couples and senior citizens who have no energy to train a cat.

7) Where to find the Japanese Bobtail

Japanese Bobtail cats are often found in breeding camps and some pet shops. They cost up to $600/£380 for a true breed.

It can be tough to find cats in this breed, as mentioned earlier. However, there is a potential for you to find a breeder if you look hard enough. The Cat Fancier's Association certifies breed clubs that breed pure cat pedigrees. Some well-known breeders can be found on Catchannel.com. The website has lots of information on getting a cat, cat health, cat behavior and more.

Even though the cat is a somewhat rare breed, it's important to ensure that breeders have the required certificates of the pedigree cat. Any breeder that is confirmed by this site will certainly be easy to trust in.

Pets4home is another site where you can easily find a Japanese Bobtail cat in the UK. You have the option to adopt or buy cats

Chapter 5: Preparations for the Japanese Bobtail

from this spot. The website emphasizes the need for certificates when it comes to purchasing the animal.

If you are planning on adopting the Japanese Bobtail cat, you can check out the following sites. PetSmart and the Pet Finder website have also listed thousands of pets available for adoption.

Be sure to also look at the listing of breeders featured a little earlier in this chapter. It is by no means an extensive list but it can give you a better idea of who is out there in terms of the best possible breeders to have.

8) Insurance and permits

Pet insurance for purebred cats costs more than those for mixed breed cats. Purebred cats are more likely to make claims for hereditary conditions that may be expensive to treat. One of the companies that provide pet insurance is Embrace Pet Insurance where you can choose a plan that fits your needs. The plan can include annual maximum, deductible and reimbursement percentages.

Some of the benefits of pet insurance is that a pet that is under a policy will be covered under breed-specific conditions, cancer treatment, diagnostic testing and imaging, surgery, hospitalization and nursing care, alternative therapies and ER and special care. This is important especially with pure breed insurance policies but it's important to do more research on the best pet insurance company to use in your country before finalizing a choice.

As you make the purchase, you need to ask yourself if you can afford cases when your cat is involved in an accident or is ill. The cost of vet visits can range from basic treatments at $280 or £170 to complex treatments costing over $3000 or £1800. Some of the recommended insurance companies include Healthy Pets, Argos Pet Insurance, Churchill Insurance, Debenhams Personal Finance and Pet Protect. These insurance companies offer personalized coverage according to the needs of the cat.

Chapter 5: Preparations for the Japanese Bobtail

Pedigree papers and the breeder's name are very important documents while purchasing the cat as well. Papers are important because some of the commercially bred kittens may develop diseases or temperament problems. Some may suffer from physical defects or come up with hereditary weaknesses. This is important for when you are trying to set up an insurance policy.

Some of the main things to check when insuring your cat include vet fees, pet insurance excess fees, lifetime covers, pet age limits and other additional benefits. Vet fees can be expensive if your pet needs treatment but with a pet insurance policy your vet fees are paid by the insurance policy.

Pet insurance policies include excess fees; it can be $50 or £30 or even more. If the visit costs you $150 or £100 you will first pay one third while the insurance company will pay the rest of what is owed. It's better to look for policies that have lower excess fees and one that meets your needs. Coverage for life policies are important so make sure you understand the benefits well. The lifetime cover insurance policy is often much more expensive than the standard cover for 12 months. A standard insurance policy covers only the first year. When your pet develops a long-term illness when the policy is renewed, the illness would be treated as an existing illness.

Few pet insurance companies have a maximum age limit for pets they will insure. Some companies may not offer coverage for pets over 10 years of age. Additional benefits may include cattery fees, and money for listing notes when a pet goes missing. Pet insurance is definitely something you should consider when buying a Japanese Bobtail cat. You will also need to get a license for having such a cat. This will be covered in the cost factor chapter of this book a little later on.

9) Pros and Cons of owning a Japanese Bobtail

Although the Japanese Bobtail is a breed that is rather new in terms of places outside Japan, it is still a cat that has a rather

Chapter 5: Preparations for the Japanese Bobtail

unique and special look that is different from what you might expect.

Naturally, you are going to have to ask yourself some questions before deciding to invest in one of these animals to see if it is really worth the purchase. So, what are the pros and cons of owning one of these animals?

a. Cons
Let us start off with the cons of owning one of these animals. **Firstly, they can be expensive due to how hard they are to find.** The fact that you'd have to spend $600 or £380 just to get a cat like this can be a big issue for some people to bear with.

Another con you should look out for does not necessarily have to do with owning but **the process of purchasing.** Due to the fact that these are such rare animals, a lot of cat breeders will claim to have these kittens when in fact they don't. Make sure to be on the look out for scam artists such as these. One way they may try to do this is by selling you cats without their papers.

The reasons why you should not buy an undocumented cat are obvious. These scammers may also try to give you fake papers for their kittens. Make sure to see that these papers are from the CFA, ACFA, or TICA. If they can't provide these documents, then it is not a Japanese Bobtail cat no matter what the breeder says.

In addition, this cat is **not for those who are out of the house for a while.** These cats tend to love attention and will become easily frustrated if they are left alone for far too much time in the day.

b. Pros
Now for some of the pros of owning these animals:

Japanese Bobtail cats are amazingly beautiful animals. – They are also available in a wide range of colors so you have many options when deciding on these animals. The Bobtail is available with a fine body that is striking and impressive. This breed of cat also has fur that is amazingly comfortable even with its short

Chapter 5: Preparations for the Japanese Bobtail

length. You will want to spend hours and hours petting this animal.

The Japanese Bobtail is very friendly to people. – This advantage makes it so it will not be too hard for a Japanese Bobtail to be kept in the house.

Along with being beautiful, these cats are also extremely smart and athletic. – This is what makes them so good at cat shows. Whenever it comes to the agility part of these cats, it shows that the Japanese Bobtail cat usually excels.

The temperament of these cats can be described as social, affectionate, and playful. – This makes this cat ideal for a family environment. A major perk of owning this animal is that although their coat is relatively long, this cat requires little grooming. They only require grooming at a moderate level.

Chapter 6: Basic Care of the Japanese Bobtail Cat

1) Introducing your kitten to your home

a. Settling in to the home
This may be an exciting time for you but cats take a longer time to adapt to the new environment. Cats are generally attached to their surroundings and change can be unsettling. Ensure your cat needs are met including easy access to food, water and a place to sleep. Others include a place to hide where the cat can sleep and hide away from the rest of the household. A raised area is advisable where your cat will sleep in a quiet environment.

Introduce the cat to the home by leaving doors open and making all rooms accessible. This will help the cat feel comfortable in his or her area. In contrast with this method, confining the cat to one room can help the cat get accustomed to the sounds and smells in the new home.

Place the litter box, bed, scratching post, food and water in a room with the cat. Surround the cat with things that smell familiar like a favorite bed, blanket or toys. Placing stuff that smell like you is another way that can make kittens more inclined to your scent.

Cat proof your home, tucking away electrical cords, ensuring all windows have secure screens and removing any poisonous houseplants that may interfere with safety. If you plan on allowing your cat to go outside, make sure you keep him/her indoors for at least two weeks. This is mainly done to familiarize the cat with the home.

There are several things that the cat needs to get accustomed to before he/she decides to venture out into other spaces in the

Chapter 6: Basic Care of the Japanese Bobtail

house. The smells and sounds around it are the first things that it must get accustomed to. There are several sounds that are new for it. Your voice, the sound of the telephone, the sound of your car starting in the driveway and all other sounds that seem quite ordinary to us are a big deal for your cat.

There are several smells, like the smell of your furniture and carpeting that it must become familiar with. It must also get used to your smell. It is through these pieces of information that the cat takes a careful look at how safe the environment is.

You need to be especially careful when taking care of the cat while moving from one house to the next. During the trip you can administer a sedative to ensure comfort throughout the journey in the cat carrier. Settling a new cat in your home is an essential part of ensuring they are comfortable with the environment. A cat that is not comfortable with their environment may run away from their new home. In this case, keep all doors and windows well shut to prevent the cat from running away.

b. Introducing the kitten to other pets
Introducing a new pet to your old pets at home can be challenging for every cat owner. It's important to have realistic expectations by recognizing and accepting the fact that you cannot force them to be friends. In this section we provide tips that work to increase your chances of success. Choosing a cat with the same activity level and personality is a good start. Another important aspect you need to know is the ages, especially because older cats may not appreciate the antiques of a kitten.

Cats are naturally territorial and can be unhappy with a newcomer. Cats hate change and a newcomer in the house can be a huge change. The cat may show displeasure by fighting with the other cat and marking their territory.

Some cats are more social than older animals that have never learned to share their territory. In such a case, slow introductions may help to prevent fearful or aggressive behavior that may develop between the new cat and current cat. The slow

Chapter 6: Basic Care of the Japanese Bobtail

introduction method takes from a few weeks to months and it needs a lot of patience on your part.

The confinement process includes allowing time for the newcomer to adjust to the new environment and situation. To do this, keep him/her in a small room with the litter box, food, water and toys for several days. Certain techniques have been successfully used to ensure the cat is comfortable in the new environment.

Feed your resident cat and the newcomer on the opposite sides of the door. This way the cats can associate something enjoyable with each other's smells. Be careful not to put the food too close to each other in case they get too upset. In time, you can gradually move the dishes closer to the door until the cats can eat calmly, standing directly on either side.

Using a pet to improve interactions with the resident and newcomer cat is another way of introducing them. Tie a toy on either side of the door and hopefully they will start battling the toys around and even battling paws. Spend plenty of time with the new kitty in the confined room without ignoring the resident cat.

Smells are far more important than appearances. Swapping the blankets or beds that cats use and gently rubbing it across the cheek of the cats or underneath the food dish can help. When the pets finally meet, they will have familiar scents. Introducing a new pet to the other should be gradual so neither animal is afraid or aggressive. Face to face contact will tell you more in the direction of the new relationship. Mutual sniffing and grooming are signs that this process is on its way to success.

In a different case, the cats may show signs of aggression, which include flattened ears, growling, splitting or crouching. You can distract them by throwing a pillow to them to reduce the tension. Such a standoff may take up to 24 hours. If the cats tend to fight repeatedly then you may need to start the process all over again. You can reduce the growing tension by having them share one litter box, keeping the resident cats' routine as it was before the newcomer and making sure they both have a safe place to escape.

Even with a dog around, the Japanese Bobtail cat is a highly co-existing character. Its ability to adapt easily with dogs is a beneficial feature. There should be no worry on the compatibility of a Japanese Bobtail kitten and a puppy, as they will develop a lasting relationship. The number of fights or brutal engagements between these cats and dogs is very minimal to rare, making them highly recommended as pet partners.

c. Introducing kittens to children
According to the American Academy of Child & Adolescent Psychiatry, pets can:

Help kids learn about compassion

Be loving beings

Support the development of self-esteem

Encourage physical activity

Help kids to be responsible and to learn important life lessons

Be links in some way to nature

Children are naturally drawn to cats but even so it's important to lay down some ground rules. An excited child can harm a smaller cat. On the other hand, injuries may occur from bites and scratches. It is important to keep kids monitored during the interactions and to teach them about handling the cat with kindness and respect.

When toddlers become more mobile they may regard a cat as an animated stuffed toy. Toddlers operate at a cat's own level and move erratically, emitting giggles and squeals. It's important to teach them the simple rules of interactions with the cat to protect both the toddler and cat together unsupervised.

Chapter 6: Basic Care of the Japanese Bobtail

Teach your child the proper way to interact from stroking the cat to avoiding the more sensitive areas around the cat's body including the belly and tail. Explain that poking, squeezing or pulling fur, tails and ears is not okay. Toddlers are extremely sociable. Make sure the cat has safe escape perches and watch the body language of cats and children; if they are worked up, separate them.

Older children are more reliable and are ready to start learning about how to care for the cat. Do not allow rough play, which may encourage the cat to use its teeth and claws, by teaching your child ways to play with the cat using safe cat toys.

Teach the difference between teasing and playing. Model proper behavior by treating your cat with affection and respect at all times. Involve your children in caring for your cat; they can replenish food and water bowls, gently brush the cat or help in keeping the litter pan clean. Teach them how to close the door, keeping them out of danger of going outside.

When it comes to associating and interacting cats with children it's important to minimize such risks. It's important to bring your cat to regular cat checkups and fecal examinations. Ensure the cat is appropriately vaccinated and is free from infectious diseases. It's important to keep the cat indoors to minimize exposure to illnesses that cause organisms such as fleas or intestinal parasites. Wash your hands after handling the cat, discourage the child from kissing the cat or even allowing the cat to lick the child's face. Keeping litter pans clean will protect the curious toddler from accessing the litter pan.

The compatibility of these Japanese Curl cats to kids is excellent. Thus, more parents prefer them for their children. Despite being extremely sensitive and gentle, it easily integrates with children. It is therefore natural to feel comfortable enough to leave the kids with your Japanese Bobtail cat. Kids tend to enjoy the experience due to how playful the cat can get. The safety of the child is also assured.

Chapter 6: Basic Care of the Japanese Bobtail

2) Basic care and routine

An established routine is essential for any cat. Routines keep the day balanced and with an established one it's important for a new cat to develop into the routine. A routine may include playtime, feeding and bath time. As the owner, having a well established routine will help your cats to be well associated, especially if you own more than two.

A routine forms the basis of the security and comfort for the cat. Older cats tend to be less capable of adapting to changes; the slightest change, however small, comes with sudden reactions.

Cat routines can be good for bonding. Most cats are drawn to their owners because of being expectant of certain thing like brushing, ear cleaning and even baths. A cat with an established routine makes it easy to detect when they are not feeling well. An ill cat may not necessarily use the same kind of routine they have established.

Some important cat routines for your cat are how often and when you play and exercise together, the consistency of diet, regular mealtimes, normal noise and activity levels in your household and morning and evening rituals for the family and the cat. Regular routines help you to plan a regular day on the weekly calendar to change the litter, buy cat food and groom your cat. A routine is an excellent way to be aware of the cat's health needs.

Note
It is tough bringing home a cat, as it can be risky when you are not certain of how it reacts with children as well as pets at home. The most common characteristic is aggression, which is prevalent among many cats. Naturally, cats are predators. Once the kittens stay behind with their mothers, there is a tendency for the kittens to be taught things like attacking or pouncing. This is merely an innate characteristic that is noticeable in all cats. Even with simple tools such as a roll of wool, the predator instinct is ever-present.

Chapter 6: Basic Care of the Japanese Bobtail

On the other hand, the Japanese Bobtail cat is absolutely unique with this aspect. Incidentally, it is accepting of all animals as well as pets in the house. Even with a dog around, the cat can live quite well with it. Its ability to adapt easily with dogs is another beneficial feature. There should be no worries about the compatibility of a Japanese Bobtail kitten and a puppy, as they will develop a lasting relationship. The number of fights or brutal engagements between these cats and dogs is very minimal to rare, making them highly recommended as pet partners.

The compatibility of these cats to kids is excellent. Thus, more parents prefer them for their children. Despite being extremely sensitive and gentle, it easily integrates itself and is most compatible with children. It is therefore natural to feel comfortable enough to leave the kids with your cat. Kids tend to enjoy the experience due to how playful the cat can get. The safety of the child is also assured.

The existence of another pet cat in the household may not always be a good thing. This is because some cat breeds do not go along well with the Japanese Bobtail. It would therefore be necessary to maintain a bit of caution to keep the peace. Its ability to dominate in situations will be evident eventually. No matter how well matched the cats may be, the Bobtail will always come out on top. The main cause for this will be the focus on seeking attention, rather than fighting for or sharing it.

Naturally, cats hold within them a social chain of command, commonly called a pecking order. The Japanese Bobtail follows the following command chain:

First, it listens to people.

Next, it listens to dogs.

Third, it listens to other cats.

Whatever the circumstance, the Bobtail will definitely be the most adaptable cat breed around.

Chapter 6: Basic Care of the Japanese Bobtail

3) Astuteness

There is little in terms of doubt when in comes to the intelligence of the Japanese Bobtail cat breed. The ease with which one can impose training or tricks is amazing. This makes it a top breed in terms of teaching complex setups and games. The most common tricks are the parlor tricks. Other simple tasks involve toilet usage, obeying commands, and so on.

Another particular attribute that comes to our attention is the curiosity of the Japanese Bobtail. The instances of peeking and prodding at 'exciting' places are numerous. As much as it may look ideal for their learning, it makes it almost impossible for you to institute brittle products as part of your interior home design. It would be disastrous to watch such a beauty being laid to waste by your brilliant cat.

The immense appreciation of heightened area by the cat means that you will expect to find them in the highest points of the house. Therefore, whenever you cannot locate them at the top of shelves or cupboards, it would only be fair to find them curled on the seats or your lap. They have no problem at all reaching these vantage points due to the extreme balance and sturdy build of the Japanese Bobtail's body. They are also relatively swift, adding to that purpose. It is rare and almost impossible to find them under tables or sofas even when there are guests around.

There are no limitations as to which environment the cat can thrive in. This adaptation actualizes the claims of the sensitivity of these cats. No specific intent is made to stick to one person as they appreciate everyone gracefully. It may therefore be useless for you to try to steer the process of integration, since they are independent. This form of malleability makes the process of training it to follow a specific schedule much simpler.

The best way that the astute Japanese Bobtail cat learns most of its tricks is by observation. The sense of observance means that they can do intelligent tasks including opening doors. Without

Chapter 6: Basic Care of the Japanese Bobtail

breaking a sweat, they will let themselves into a room by purposely turning the knobs. It will depend on you to lock them out of those rooms you may consider dangerous or sensitive. There are various features that define how intelligent they are, and with continuous hybridization, there is no limit to the functions they perform.

Being the owner of such an intelligent breed as a Japanese Bobtail cat comes with unique benefits. The days of dull moments in the household are definitely gone with such a pet companion as a cat.

4) The Most Charming Cat

For the stay-at-home individual, the Japanese Bobtail breed is definitely the choice for you. Admirably social and active, it forms a good companion. Its beauty is just a portion of its antics to attract your attention. Be assured they will not be annoying, but rather entertaining and lovely.

The manner in which he or she quickly understands what pleases the owner makes it simpler because the actions will come very often. The best example is shown in the chasing of a roll of thread. The family also matters, with a constant input to please everyone. With the consistent entertainment, it will be difficult for you to take your attention off the cat.

The instances the cat will remain in a bored state are quite few, as they have a way of keeping themselves entertained. There is a huge momentum in its actions, with a natural demand to keep the social interaction by constantly creating play.

It is natural to lose interest in such antics after some time, but this does not mean you should grow impatient. So, what is the right reaction from a pet owner? Foremost, expect a clear expression of dissatisfaction from the Japanese Bobtail cat when that interest is lacking. They definitely are not annoying or noisy but they are rather vocal.

Chapter 6: Basic Care of the Japanese Bobtail

Nature demands of them to be sensitive, with a unique response to such instances. The response may be exceptionally shrill. Depending on the situation, the Japanese Bobtail will call or purr at various intensities. For example, after coming home, the typical reaction will be excitement purrs and following you around wherever you choose to go.

The Bobtail cat has a sincere feeling of affection towards its owner, something that any individual would find welcoming and a sure sense of loyalty. They also enjoy the company, play and love that come with it. The most interesting bit is the manner in which it will react to an individual's temperament.

It's opposite reactions to sadness and feelings of frustration will often prove beneficial and rehabilitating to the owner. Otherwise, it is important to note that there is no option for it to abandon you.

Does your cat need a friend? Research shows that cats that grow up in pairs are the happiest. So, if you want to get your cat a companion, you can ask your breeder for the most suitable option.

How pet friendly is your home? The Japanese Bobtail is the perfect apartment cat. So even if you live in an apartment, it will not really matter. However, if there are any restrictions with respect to keeping pets in your apartment, you must be aware of it. In addition to that you must make sure that you also have access to pet stores and vets in the area that you live in. If you feel that your home is inconvenient for your pet, you might want to rethink the option of owning a cat.

Your Lifestyle: If you feel like your cat will not have enough company while it is at home then do not even think of purchasing a cat. Japanese Bobtails crave attention and can have several health complications if they are not given ample love and affection.

Once all these issues have been sorted, you can prepare your home for the Japanese Bobtail. You can consider the option of

Chapter 6: Basic Care of the Japanese Bobtail

adopting. However, before you do, here are some things that you must be able to provide your adopted pet with:

Necessary care in case of reported abuse

Vet assistance if it is ill or old

A separate room or enclosure to protect him/her and other pets at home

Constant care to help it adapt

The necessary nutrition if he/she has health issues.

If you are confident of being able to provide all of the above, adoption is the noblest thing that you can do for your pet. Give him/her a loving home where it will be able to learn to live a life of dignity and happiness.

Chapter 7: Synopsis of the Japanese Bobtail Cat Character

For easier understanding of the true character of this cat, the listing below will undoubtedly be of help. The rating of each attribute is out of five. The results here are an average of the response given by most Japanese Bobtail owners. It is thus upon you to choose it over other cats breeds.

Character attribute	Rating
Fondness towards Owner	5/5
Malleability	5/5
Playfulness	5/5
Congruency with Other Cats	4/5
Congruency with Dogs	4/5
Congruency with Children	4/5
Intelligence	5/5

Connecting with the Japanese Bobtail

There is a list of small to large tasks to engage your cat in as soon as it arrives. This is to create an atmosphere of understanding and getting to know you and its new environment so everyone in the room will be happy with what is happening.

Chapter 7: Synopsis of the Japanese Bobtail Cat Character

a. The First Few Hours
Attempt to reach and cuddle the cat for its first feel of you. This is sometimes necessary if it feels nervous and comes to you. Regular visits to the cat are recommended to build on trust. Calling out to the cat in a soft voice while sitting in a low position would be more appealing and a better chance at bonding. Spacing the number of times you leave him/her alone in a room is fundamental too. The actual recognition may take a while, and as the owner, you are not expected to lose your patience. Allow time for proper recognition to take place.

Visits by children in your home or family should be in the company of an older individual. This may be limited to the first few days of the introduction into the family. The excitement from kids during such periods may be overwhelming, leading to slight injuries to them if they unsettle it. There should be adequate supervision at all times.

b. Create time for your cat
The Japanese Bobtail adores attention. There is a likelihood of the cat feeling depressed if he or she feels less attended to. It is therefore proper to create time for them. It may not necessarily involve any sort of play, but rather having your presence felt in that room. In the case where there is more than one person in that home, the visits should come in turns to offer more options and improve on its co-existence with multiple persons. Remain in the room as long as possible to create some form of association.

c. Playtime
It is possible to develop a good connection with the cat through playtime. The most common sign is to see that the cat is not hiding so much. The only way that a cat would want to show that it is ready for you is by rubbing off one's scent on you. This slowly begins with occasional rubs against your legs. This affectionate nature may not be met with a similar response if you try to touch them.

Chapter 7: Synopsis of the Japanese Bobtail Cat Character

Employing toys is a nice way of initiating real contact with the cat. The best toy that evidently works is the use of a string or a shoelace. By running it along the floor, you tempt the predatory instinct in the cat to pounce on it. The cat will thus find it difficult not to play along. Immediately, the surroundings are clear and there is a clear connection building, there should be obvious fun and endless play with you.

d. Special Circumstances
The heaviest challenge lies with the owner while trying to establish that bond. Whether there is a child or another pet in the house, it should be your task to intelligently introduce them to the cat. The methods will vary too. There is a certain model that the Japanese Bobtail cat operates on, with the unique situation involving a grown cat. As described before, those steps can ensure a smooth transition in the bonding process. Making the process as comfortable as possible is recommended.

Chapter 8: When a Japanese Bobtail is Pregnant

1) Reaching Puberty

When a male cat reaches puberty, he is known as a Tom. On the other hand, a female cat that hits puberty is known as the queen. Puberty in male cats sets in when they are about 6 or 9 months old. Breeding a male cat is only a good idea if the litter that he came from was healthy and was of a good size. His mother should not have had any complications while giving birth. You can ask your breeder for this information before you buy your cat.

The female cat will experience multiple cycles of heat during the breeding season. This season usually starts in January or February and continues until October or November. The temperature during this season and the ratio between light and dark hours will play a significant role in your cat's heat cycle.

A female cat in the Japanese Bobtail breed is ready to bear kittens at the age of 7 to 9 months. She will remain fertile for at least 9 years after she hits puberty. Only if your female cat comes from a healthy litter and a healthy mother should you consider breeding as a good option. You can have your cat tested for the possibility of genetic disorders and illnesses to understand how safe or reasonable it is to choose the option of breeding.

Most female cats will show obvious signs before the actual heat sets in. You will see her roll around on the floor, rub herself against objects and also meow persistently. However, she will not allow a tom to mount her. This is not a sign of pain as most owners presume. It is just your cat's hormones raging. This heat cycle should last for about 8 days. The interval between one heat cycle and another is usually about 10 days. So expect your cat to

Chapter 8: When a Japanese Bobtail is Pregnant

exhibit this behavior at least twice a month during the breeding season.

The hormonal changes that take place in the cat's body in this period are tremendous. While estrogen causes the onset of the heat cycle, progesterone takes over when she is pregnant. As the level of estrogen increases, the heat cycle will intensify. Once the level of estrogen drops, the heat cycle ends. This rise and fall of estrogen will only end when she is mated. Remember, a typical pregnancy can last for nine weeks and result in a litter of three to five Japanese Bobtail cats. Be sure to watch for this when a female is pregnant.

2) Finding the Right Mate

Cats are extremely sensitive creatures. Most often, they will be able to choose their own mates when you take them to the breeder. You can always take a look at good cats that you can utilize in the event that yours has not been spayed or neutered. This is good if you want to produce additional cats if you have an interest in this.

For these typical cats, it is not necessary for you to pick another of the same breed for mating (even if it is the best way to ensure that the cat will have the same look you expect from it). You can even out-cross the cat with another breed that has either the same length of hair as your cat or something else. Don't worry if you cannot find a good Japanese Bobtail to breed your Bobtail with; after all, it is not always easy to find the best Bobtails out there.

You must always take a queen to the tom for breeding, as she will not be too sensitive to these environmental changes during the mating process. The actual mating does not last for more than 4 minutes. Once this is over, the queen will break free by striking the male with her paw and turning away. The after reaction of the female is just cleaning herself after rolling and thrashing for a while. The after reaction may last up to 9 minutes.

Chapter 8: When a Japanese Bobtail is Pregnant

If you are interested in producing a litter, you may have to allow your cat to be mated multiple times. With a single mating, there is only a 50% chance of your cat getting pregnant. Studies show that female cats will allow up to 30 matings at intervals of 5 minutes each. One interesting fact about cats in general is that while each kitten has one father, the fathers of the kittens in a single litter may not have the same father. This is true because of the multiple mating processes. As a result, your litter may have several varieties of kitten, depending upon the cats that your queen has mated with.

If your cat is pregnant, you will see the apparent abdomen size by the 16th day of pregnancy. If you are not experienced with cats, an ultrasound can help you decide if your cat is pregnant or not. There is an easy way to check if your cat is pregnant or not. If the uterus feels stringy, it means that your cat might be pregnant. By the 20th day of pregnancy, you can actually feel the kitten fetuses in the abdomen of the queen when she is relaxed.

Besides checking for pregnancy, ultrasound is also a useful tool to check if the development of the fetuses is normal. You can perform an ultrasound from the 26th day of pregnancy until the end of pregnancy. Enlargement and a pinkish tinge of the mammary glands will be observed as the pregnancy progresses. A pregnancy may last for about 63 days, a total of about nine weeks although it may be a week longer in some cases.

3) Important Tips and Guidelines

The pregnancy period is a very delicate one. You must ensure that you take the best care of your Japanese Bobtail to have a healthy litter and also a safe delivery. Here are a few things to keep in mind while caring for a pregnant cat:
Morning sickness is common in cats. Your vet will be able to provide you with assistance if this persists.

Your pregnant cat may also reduce her food consumption by the third week of pregnancy.

Chapter 8: When a Japanese Bobtail is Pregnant

Overfeeding and weight gain during pregnancy can lead to complications during labor.

The food that you give your queen must be highly nutritious. Protein and calcium are a must. However, never provide any supplements unless recommended by a vet.

Your cat must be kept indoors during the last 15 days of pregnancy. This helps you ensure that she does not give birth elsewhere.

During your cat's pregnancy, you must make sure that you visit the vet regularly. The most important time for your veterinarian visit is during the last two weeks of pregnancy.

4) Is my Japanese Bobtail in Labor?

There are some sure shot signs that will tell you if your beautiful Japanese Bobtail cat is ready to give birth. Here are some signs that you must look out for:

Your cat will begin to nest.

Her body temperature will drop to about 99 F. This is less than the typical 101.5 F that she would normally have.

She will start lactating.

Her appetite will reduce and she will not have an interest in eating no matter what you try doing.

She will show extreme behavior. She will either become extremely affectionate or she will just become entirely reclusive.

5) Preparing for Birth

The one phase where you will experience maximum anxiety is when your Bobtail actually gets ready to give birth. If you are not prepared, you will just end up fumbling and jeopardizing the

Chapter 8: When a Japanese Bobtail is Pregnant

health of your kitty. Here are some things that you must keep handy when your cat is in the last two weeks of her pregnancy:

A sturdy cardboard box or a kittening box available at pet stores.

Surgical gloves.

A syringe or eyedropper to remove secretions from the nose and mouth.

Cotton thread or dental floss for the umbilical cord ties.

Antiseptic for the umbilical stumps.

Scissors.

Clean and fresh towels.

The vet's number.

Milk replacer for kittens.

Emergency contact numbers.

Now, all you need to do is prepare for the actual birth. When your cat is in the last week of her pregnancy, place the kittening box in a quiet spot. This spot should be warm and completely draft free. Place your cat's favorite blanket and some toys in this box to encourage her to sleep there.

The bedding that you choose for this kittening box should be comfortable for the kittens and shouldn't snag their claws. This bedding must be changed regularly after the birth of the kittens.

6) Danger signs

In case you observe one or more of the following symptoms, make sure you call your vet right away:

Lack of appetite in your queen for 24 hours or more

The temperature is high and continues to stay elevated

She becomes lethargic

She has unpleasant smelling discharge from her vagina

These are signs that something might have gone wrong during the delivery. They also indicate postnatal stress in your cat and must be treated at the earliest.

7) Things you must not do during pregnancy

Never use any flea powder or medicine without consulting your doctor first.

Do not allow your cat to take any medication without a valid prescription.

Do not use antiseptics suitable for humans. These products, although mild on our skin, may burn your cat's delicate skin.

Avoid handling the kittens too much. There are chances that your cat will disown or even kill the kittens if intruders threaten them. Allow the kittens and the mother to bond.

Do not allow your cat to roam around. Cats can get pregnant within 2 weeks of delivery, so keep her in confinement for a while.

Do not de-sex your cat until after 7 weeks of the kitten's birth.

Taking care of a pregnant cat is a huge responsibility. If you are not sure of how to go about it, you can look for a shelter or a veterinary hospital where the cats will be taken care of until the kittens are born. Once you have the kittens, you can decide if you want to keep them in your home or find them another loving home to live in.

Chapter 9: Training the Japanese Bobtail

A well-trained cat is easy to maintain and look after. An ill-mannered cat can stress the owner. For example, litter box training an untrained cat may end up in a mess. A well-trained cat is able to use the litter box, keeping the house clean.

The fashionable look and unique qualities of the Japanese Bobtail are great in their own right. The cat is also very easy to enjoy around the house as it can be a rather fun and enjoyable companion. These cats enjoy interacting with their human families as much as with other cats.

Japanese Bobtails are very smart and engaging in lifting our spirits but so silly if not trained on their boundaries as they jump and climb everywhere and anywhere they please. They like seeking attention anyway. Unlike dogs that relax pretty much on the floor, these silly felines can jump from the top of doors to the floor in the room and then to the kitchen as if they want to help you do the dishes. This is the reason why it is important to train and manage your cat to fit your personal needs.

The Japanese Bobtail is trainable in different areas including that ever-sensitive process of litter box training. Here we will discuss some of the main tips you can use for litter box training, leash training and teaching tricks.

1) Litter box training

Buy a litter box that will be comfortable for the cat. Buy litter that is not too rough for the cat, as this may discourage the cat. There are different types of litter to choose from, which are generally fine for all cats. Perfumed litter and scoopable litter are some of the litter available in general stores. As the cat grows older, you will need to switch litters, especially if it starts eating the litter.

Chapter 9: Training the Japanese Bobtail

Kittens can become ill from ingesting large quantities of litter; those made from clay are especially lethal to any aged cat.

Cats have a natural instinct to eliminate in sand or soil. With kittens, they learn mainly from observing their mother. If you have a new kitten, they will need guidance on where to eliminate and the use of the litter boxes. Training on litter can be done with a kitten as young as 3 weeks to 4 weeks of age.

It is important to make sure your kitten knows the location of the litter box in his/her new surroundings. Ensure that the litter box is not placed in a noisy area or places with high traffic like the kitchen, as cats enjoy their privacy. Introducing them to the litter box will be done manually by placing the kitten in the litter box for them to get used to it. Teach the kitten how to scratch on the litter by placing the front paws inside; this will give it confidence.

Place the cat in the litter box at different times when they would normally go to the bathroom, such as in the morning, after meals, playing and waking up from their nap. Most cats will make the adjustments to a new litter box without any problems.

When accidents happen, do not scold or yell at the cat; instead, clean up the accident with an enzyme cleaner to remove stains and odors. Yelling and scolding will end up confusing your cat, which may slow down the litter box training. If you notice more accidents with a bout of diarrhea, consult your veterinarian to rule out any foreseen medical problems.

Be sure to provide a treat if your cat is capable of using the bathroom the right way the first time around. This is to give off a reward stating that you are pleased with the cat and that you are comfortable with whatever it is that the cat is doing.

You should provide one litter box per cat plus one extra just to be safe. Some cats prefer to use one litter box to urinate and another to defecate in. It may seem excessive to have more than one litter box but cats can be choosy creatures, which may increase the chances of small accidents in the house. Sometimes your cat is

Chapter 9: Training the Japanese Bobtail

comfortable with just one box but it never hurts to be prepared just to be safe.

Choosing the right size of litter box is essential. Kittens require a smaller size that they can be able to climb into without much effort. Self-cleaning litter boxes are also available, which save on clean up time, though some are noisy. A hooded box will concentrate the odor and should be cleaned daily.

Cleanliness is an important factor for cats and they may avoid a litter box that is not clean. Scoop the litter box at least once per day and wash the litter box and change the litter once a week. Keep off the strong smelling disinfectants that may affect the cat's superior sense of smell. Training a new cat or kitten how to use a litter box is not an easy thing, so reward them with treats when they get it right and see the difference.

Training a cat requires much patience and perseverance to bring about performance and tricks. It is advisable for you to adapt a kitten as young as three months old and start training him/her so as to achieve satisfying results in performance. Upon acquiring your kitten, don't allow it full run of the house. Try to contain him/her to one room, preferably the one you spend most of your time in, so that you can watch over it.

Immediately carry it without delay to the litter box if your kitten accidentally pees or poops where not needed.

Cats and kittens don't like using heavily soiled litter boxes, so ensure that the litter box is clean. You can thoroughly wash the litter box once a week.

Finally, litter training requires patience, as the cat is learning a new thing. Be patient and not pushy during this process. For the new cat, comfort is important and for them it may take longer. The Japanese Bobtail cat is one of the most intelligent cat breeds around and learning how to use the litter box will be an easy process.

2) Leash training

Teaching a cat to walk on a harness and leash is a great way to let your cat enjoy the outdoors while ensuring they are safe. It is not something that a Japanese Bobtail may be happy with at first but over time the cat will become more comfortable with it.

Outdoor walks can reduce obesity and boredom-related behavior that develops due to under exercise. Because cats may easily escape a collar, it's not a safe alternative. Patience is a virtue when strapping the cat to a harness. Leash training, just like other training related to pet animals, will take time. Here we will discuss the process of leash training.

a. Equipment
A good harness must be well fitted for the cat, designed for cats and must be comfortable for the cat to wear. It should be practical for the cat and lightweight - made of either cloth or nylon. Chain and leather leashes are too heavy for a cat. Attach the leash with a collar identification tag.

Leave the harness near the cat's food or favorite sleeping spot for several days. This will give the cat feelings of contentment when they see the leash. Another way is to let the cat sniff the harness by holding it close to them.

b. Acclimating the cat to the leash
This process needs to be a slow process, as rushing may cause the cat to shy away from wearing the harness. Place the harness on the cat, which is best done when the cat is relaxed to avoid any type of agitation. As you hold the harness against the cat's neck, offer treats as you lay the harness and do so as it sniffs the treat too. If your cat does not appreciate being held or restrained, get the cat used to handling. You can do this by keeping a favorite toy close by and holding it firmly but gently for a few seconds. Use soft praises while holding it and giving him/her treats. Repeat this exercise often for several days while practicing handling the cat's legs and feet.

Chapter 9: Training the Japanese Bobtail

Drape the harness over the cat's shoulders and down his/her chest between his/her front legs. Introduce this new feeling as the cat is sniffing and eating treats, work until you can snap the harness on it over his/her neck and shoulder area between his/her front legs, continuing to distract with treats.

Put the harness on the cat but do not attach the leash immediately. While distracting the cat with treats, adjust the harness to fit the cat, making sure only two fingers can fit between the cat and harness. Repeat this daily, and as the cat seems more relaxed, increase the time when the harness is on. Remove the harness if the cat seems upset.

Now it's time to attach the leash. Place your cat in an empty room, making sure nothing can snag the leash. Distract your cat with treats and as it walks around the room be sure to keep an eye out for anything that may snag, as this may scare it. Repeat this for several days until the cat becomes comfortable.

After realizing the cat is comfortable and relaxed with the leash while dragging it, slowly and gently hold the leash, not pulling, while it walks around the house. Praise it often and give treats and continue practicing this step for several days.

c. Going outside
After the successful leash training process, you may proceed to go with the cat outside. However, you can also direct the cat as he/she walks around the house. When you're outside it may be easier to direct the cat towards the direction you want them to head to.

Once you're outside, the excitement of the outdoors may overwhelm your cat. You can encourage the cat to walk along with you by using a sweet, soft voice, dropping a treat while you're walking, and applying pressure on the leash if the cat goes a different direction. Keep it close to avoid any accidents.

Do not leave the leash on the cat tied to something while you are away, as the cat may get tangled and get hurt.

Chapter 9: Training the Japanese Bobtail

3) Teaching the cat tricks

Cats are intelligent and capable of being taught new tricks. It is advisable to start teaching tricks to kittens because they are more energetic at that time. A cat can learn different tricks from dancing, standing, clapping and many more. In this chapter, we will discuss some of the tips that have stood out and are successful. Although kittens are most recommended for teaching new tricks, here we explore options on how to teach older cats new tricks. For those who have adopted or bought older cats, this section will be an important part in terms of interactions.

Communication
Animal behavior experts say that cats can be trained by a pattern of reinforced treats. In psychology, the term used is conditioned response. Certain behavioral patterns can be established in this theory, like when cats respond to the opening of a can or even the sound of clapping on their food plate. The process of training your cat will also depend on how well you communicate with each other. Engaging your cat in conversation on a daily basis is the fastest way to teach your cat the tone of your voice.

Body language
Cats communicate mostly through their body language and it is important to be able to recognize the meaning of each move. This can include tail position, reading the eyes, the ears and leg rubbing. The tail position of a cat can tell you so much about their emotions. The tail of the cat acts as a mood barometer and provides balance for the cat. You may notice at times that the tail of the cat is held loosely upright when walking; this shows confidence and contentment.

If you find your cat flicking its tail upright in your direction, it is giving you a warm greeting. If it whips it from side to side or thumps it on the floor, it means he/she is agitated or angry, so find out what is making it angry. If the cat puffs the tail, he/she may be spooked by something or someone and is receptive by calming it down.

Chapter 9: Training the Japanese Bobtail

Read the eyes when a cat looks at you. If the eyes are dilated, it means he/she is nervous or agitated and requires some space. The eyes of a cat are the most stunning features and they communicate a lot of emotion. A cat's ears move when the cat is being receptive and you will notice that the ears look forward and slightly outwards. A ready to fight cat flattens its ears against its head.

When you find your cat rubbing against your legs or brushing its cheekbone against your hand, it means that he/she is marking you. It sets a sense of belonging to the part of the cat, a type of feline flattery. In some ways, it may be translated as marking its territory against other animals, either outside or within the household.

Sounds
Different sounds can also be translated into communication. These sounds include the meow, purr, chirp and trill. Meow sounds may be a sign of demanding something. This could be food or daily walks, it depends on the need at that particular time.

The purr sound happens when they are receiving an end message. It may also be due to the discomfort of visiting the veterinary clinic. Cats purr with their mouths closed. The chirp sound happens when they see prey or flies in the house. They may make this noise when they see certain animals such as birds, squirrels and other small creatures. A trill is between a meow and purr and is a greeting. Other sounds you will hear from your cat include growling, chattering, yowling, hissing and wailing. It will be important to master these noises for efficient communication with your cat.

4) Training a cat to learn new tricks

After learning about the different communication strategies that you can relate to, now you can start teaching your new pet new tricks. Tricks include sitting up, come here, jump, shake hands and waving. All this will require adequate communication between you and your cat.

Chapter 9: Training the Japanese Bobtail

Bonding with your cat will be cemented during this period of training. One thing you need to understand is the aspect of appraisal by use of treats. Treats are often used to motivate cats, as they will enjoy some fine things to eat every once in a while. The Japanese Bobtail is an intelligent cat and is a fast learner when it comes to figuring out new tricks. Its playful nature will provide a better atmosphere of learning new tricks. Most of the showcased cats in cat shows go through intensive training.

Animal psychologists advise owners to train their cats for a few minutes during the day. Training your cat has important benefits like stimulating the body and mind and keeping your cat healthy. Spending time together will strengthen your bond. Here are some helpful tips to help you as you teach your cat new tricks.

Use tasty treats. By identifying your cat's favorite treat you can follow these basic steps of positive reinforcement training. First you have to get the attention of your cat by holding the treat to your cat's nose. Move it in different directions on its face and chin and as he/she follows your movements, you will notice the butt will go down. When its bottom hits the floor, praise your cat and offer the treat. Repeat this several times if your cat does not completely hit the floor. Repetition is the best way to remind your cat what you have already taught it.

Using a Clicker
Clicker training is considered the easiest way to teach cats some new tricks. The first goal in clicker training is to establish a simple form of communication between the trainer and the cat. It allows the cat to understand what specific noises are saying. This allows you as the trainer to pick just about anything the cat does and encourage it to repeat the same thing or do it on command.

Clicker training can also be efficiently used during litter box training. When the cat uses the litter box in the correct way, use the clicker to appreciate and encourage it to do it again. Although there are many different clickers on the market, one can use a pen that resembles the same noise. Even in cat training, practice makes perfect.

Don't Punish
Cats do not respond well to punishment. They run away rather than learning from their behavior. Depending on the cat's attitude, a punishment can cause that cat to be less likely to want to be around other people. This problem may cause and alleviate stress levels in your cat, which in some cases may trickle down to their normal cat behaviors. Eliminating outside the litter box or even compulsive grooming are some of the signs of a stressed cat.

Provide a safe environment when teaching new tricks as cats respond to distractions. This may eventually slow the process of teaching new tricks to your cat. A well-trained cat is enjoyable to have and will amaze you with newly found tricks each time.

Cats do most things on their own but again they are quick learners. Just like dogs, cats are trained to sit, dance and even shake their paws. In order to train your cat to learn these tricks, first of all, identify your cat's personality and energy level. Most importantly, have some fun in it and have the tricks that will motivate your cat to continue training because if the cat gets frustrated, he/she won't continue and you definitely wouldn't achieve your goal.

Tricks to get your cat to sit well – Hold a treat above your cat's head and mouth and then command him/her to sit down so that all four paws and bottom are on the floor. As it tries to struggle to eat the treat, place the back of your hand on its head to guide him/her down so that he/she gains balance and after that, give him/her the treat to eat. Doing this repeatedly will get your Japanese Bobtail to understand what the it has to do when you say "sit down."

Shake a hand- take the paw of your cat and shake it while saying your chosen command, such as shake hands. Repeat this exercise and soon the cat will respond lovingly to your paw shake. The paw shake is a great way to show off to your visitors.

Jumping and dancing – Hold the treat some inches above his/her mouth and say "jump" or put the treat on a toothpick or stick and hold the stick vertically in front of your cat's face and tell it to get it. As the cat tries to sniff the treat, take it away from him/her. When he/she can no longer stand bipedal or falls on the floor, praise him/her and give the treat so that he/she feels rewarded for the efforts made.

Roll over – This is the trick to train your cat to lie down. First place your cat on a table and hold the treat under the table. Guide your cat to lie down by saying the command "lie down", then once your cat can follow the command, take the treat and stand up over its head and command it to roll. This is not easy and so your cat might need some time to learn this trick.

Rewarding
Rewarding is the most motivating factor while training your cat. If you are using food and your cat does not respond, maybe he/she is not hungry. Try another tactic like praising or patting and this can work. Do the training session on a regular basis so that your cat can get used to and learn the tricks quickly. Choosing the right method will depend on your relationship with your cat. In many instances, cats with a healthy relationship with the owner are found to be more receptive to commands. As we discussed above, the aspect of communication between you and the cat are important for developing a bond between you.

In conclusion, training a cat is an easy task by using the simple principles. Whether it is litter box training, leash training or teaching new tricks, communication is an important aspect. As the cat owner you need to understand the cat's temperament. This will go a long way in your relationship.

Chapter 10: Grooming the Japanese Bobtail

Cat grooming is a professional job. Professional expertise can only ensure that the cats are hygienically perfect and look beautiful too. There can be many diseases and infections that can be caused by the fur of the cat. Therefore, the owners of the cats should use state of the art methodologies to clean and groom their cats. There are professional cat grooming centers that can do the job more conveniently and quickly for you.

The owners of the cats can also groom their cats, provided they have the required knowledge and equipment to groom, clean and beautify their cats. As most of the owners love their cats to bits, they prefer to groom their cats themselves. The Japanese Bobtail cat is one of the most loved breeds of cats and requires special care and techniques in order to groom it.

The Japanese Bobtail has a coat that will vary in length based on each individual cat. You might find some with short coats or others with semi-long coats. Either way, you need to make sure you take good care of your cat no matter what type of cat you are going to stick with.

Grooming is a very essential part of owning a Japanese Bobtail Cat. It is to make your cat look brilliant. However, there are several reasons besides the physical appearance of your pet to ensure that you include grooming sessions. You accomplish five things by grooming your Japanese Bobtail once a week or so:

You get to dedicate time to spend with your cat.

You help to maintain the health of the cat by removing loose hairs and debris that the cat may choke on in the process of pruning itself.

You are able to keep an eye out for infections, cuts and other skin disorders.

Chapter 10: Grooming the Japanese Bobtail

Your cat's coat is your responsibility. You can maintain the lustrous coat of the Japanese Bobtail by bathing, brushing and cleaning the coat on a scheduled basis.

You can take care of your own belongings and prevent injuries to people by maintaining the claws of your Japanese Bobtail.

If you are not sure of how to go about the grooming process, several professionals are willing to help you with it. You can approach cat-grooming specialists and have maintenance contracts according to your convenience. Most of them will be specialized in dealing with cats and can be trusted to give your kitty the best.

1) Benefits of Grooming a Japanese Bobtail cat

There are several benefits associated with grooming such a cat as this. It does not only beautify the cat but also looks after a lot of health and care issues related to the cats. Here is a brief list of the benefits associated with the grooming of Japanese Bobtail cats:

- Grooming of the cats helps in improving the muscle tones.

- It helps to stimulate the skin, which in return produces oil. The oil produced gives a healthy shine to the coat.

- The Japanese Bobtail is not known to shed as much as other breeds but it's still essential for you to remove any dead hairs that are on the cat's body. If you brush your cat while it is malting then you can easily remove the loose hairs off of the coat. This is a process that makes the shedding function a little easier to manage.

- This practice also helps in preventing the formation of hairballs on the coat of the cat. If you do not groom your cat on a regular basis, then it can lead to certain severe problems like forming hairballs on the fur, which can catch more germs and bacteria.

Chapter 10: Grooming the Japanese Bobtail

- The grooming session also gibes the master or the attendant to have a close physical look at the cat. Sometimes, there can be serious injuries or infection, which is not noticed in the normal routine until they are taken for a grooming session.

- In the grooming session, the attendant can have a close look at the overall body including ears, eyes, nose, and mouth, ear mites, checking for fleas, or any formation of lumps or bumps on the body of the cat.

- The grooming session can be very therapeutic for the concerned parties, the cat and the attendant. Both the attendant and the cat can develop a good bond between them.

Cats can be difficult to groom for the first time. There is a need to develop a good sense of bonding between the two concerned parties. The good bonding can be developed with the newly born kitten. It is a natural tendency of the new kitten that it always responds in a positive way to any love or affection shown towards it. Once the cat matures or a new master adopts it, then it can be a really daunting job to get accustomed with the new cat.

Japanese Bobtails especially have this tendency. In such circumstances, a nice and friendly grooming session can be an excellent means to developing a good relationship between the master and his/her cat. The first grooming session is the most important when either the cat or the master should strive to develop a bond.

If both of them fail the first time in developing an understanding, then it can get extremely difficult to carry on a smooth grooming session the next time. Any nasty surprises from either of the two could lead to a bad relationship, which can be extremely difficult to minimize if the attendant does not handle things very well, no matter what the conditions might be.

2) Equipment needed for grooming a cat

As cat grooming is a detailed process, plenty of sophisticated equipment is needed. Here is some of the equipment needed for grooming the Japanese Bobtail or any other cat that needs to be groomed on occasion:

- Clippers
- Blades
- Combs
- Brushes
- Shampooing products
- Soaps

3) Handling and Safety Pointers

The health and safety of both the cat and the person taking care of the grooming process is important. Dealing with cats or any kind of animals could lead to fatal injuries. Cat bites can be extremely painful and can have long lasting effects. It can cause certain fatal infections that can take time to cure or sometimes can get worse. Therefore, in order to groom a Japanese Bobtail cat, safety should be the main concern.

Make sure you take all the safety precautions before beginning with the cleaning and grooming of your cat. The personality traits of both the cat and the person doing the grooming process should be carefully assessed. There are a lot of cat lovers that are also allergic to the fur of the cats. Therefore, they are highly advised to wear gloves before starting the process. This would either eliminate or at least reduce any threat of catching any allergy from the cat.

Chapter 10: Grooming the Japanese Bobtail

Furthermore, the cats as well have some dodgy personality traits that can be of concern. They can have sharp nails or teeth, which can cause injuries to the person servicing the cat. Safety equipment like gloves or safety jackets is highly advised.

You can also wear safety equipment as needed in order to protect yourself during the grooming process. The cat can be made to wear a mouth mask and small pads over its paws. This precautionary measure can significantly reduce the chances of any possibility of physical damage caused to the attendant or the service provider.

Cats of this breed tend to have different temperaments. They have the tendency to get violent during their cleaning or grooming sessions. Some cats do not enjoy their grooming sessions and can attack. On the other hand, some Japanese Bobtail cats can remain completely calm throughout the session.

You should try to divert the attention of violent cats. This can be presented with their most loved playing equipment while the attendant can easily carry on with the grooming job. The owner or master of the Japanese Bobtail cat is the best person to judge the traits and temperament of his/her cat. He/she knows when the cat gets violent and what activities can amuse it the most. He/she also has an idea of how to control the cat during the grooming session.

Therefore, if you are looking to get your cat groomed by a professional, make sure that you as the owner of the cat are also present throughout the session. It is true that the professionals should have all the tactics to control the cat, but the cat in a new environment like a cat-grooming parlor can easily get violent, especially when he/she does not see his/her master around.

Hygiene and sanitation of the Japanese Bobtail or any other cat is also of utmost consideration. Neglecting any of these aspects could lead to incurable diseases. Either the attendant doing the servicing of cats at home or a commercial cat-grooming center should carry on with the process while maintaining the required standards.

Chapter 10: Grooming the Japanese Bobtail

The equipment used should be properly sterilized before commencing the grooming session. It is also highly recommended that the equipment used once should be immediately sterilized after the grooming session and once before commencing with a new grooming session.

Furthermore, the same equipment should not be used for different animals, which are normally a major concern at the pets grooming centers. The reason for not mixing the grooming equipment is the different traits of different animals. The equipment used for washing should also be of top quality with no substandard goods. People who love their cats know very well how valuable their cat's skin is for them. Ordinary shampoo or bathing equipment could result in severe fur loss or can also cause the reduction in the quality of its hair and skin.

4) Can a Tranquilizer Work?

A tranquilizer is not required when taking care of the Japanese Bobtail during the grooming process. Still, some people might suggest that you need to use it.

A professional groomer might suggest that a tranquilizer is needed. However, this is not recommended due to the potential adverse effects that may come about.

If your groomer says that you need to provide a tranquilizer to your cat in order to get it groomed then you should take the cat elsewhere. You have to allow your cat to relax on its own in order to ensure that the grooming process is as easy to handle as possible.

The key is to allow the cat to relax for a bit. Make sure that the cat rests for a while and allow it to keep calm so it will not be overly active during the grooming process. This is safer to manage than just giving the cat some kind of medication that it may not handle well. Remember: if you hear from a groomer that it needs a tranquilizer then you are better off taking your Japanese

Chapter 10: Grooming the Japanese Bobtail

Bobtail to another groomer or to just take care of the process on your own.

5) The Basics of Grooming for Japanese Bobtail Cats

The coat on the Japanese Bobtail cat is rather relaxed and easy to brush through. It can vary in terms of length but it will be silky and easy to brush along if you use the right comb.

It is typically best to have a comb on hand to brush the cat's coat every week or two. This is regardless of when in the year you are taking care of the grooming process. The coat doesn't become thicker or thinner for the most part but it will still require plenty of brushing every week.

Look for brushes and combs that are suitable for the cat's coat based on the length of its hair. While a brush with long bristles can work for cats with longer haired coats, you might want to make sure you are careful when getting your cat's hair in check. The undercoat is not all that thick and should be rather easy to comb through.

In addition, make sure you watch for how you comb the hair. Don't go too far towards the coat and don't try scratching it too hard. If you don't do it right then you might cause skin rashes and scratches on your cat's skin, thus putting it at a risk of developing an infection in the worst possible case.

This isn't going to be all that hard to do but you should at least make sure you keep any dead hair bits out of the way. This is to keep the coat as clear and comfortable as possible.

Always check for flea excreta by looking at different spots that might be found around the hair. If you see any fleas then you will need to give your cat a proper bath to ensure that there are no troubles coming from the fleas. Taking care of the bath as soon as possible is critical as it will be harder to get rid of all these fleas if you don't provide a good bath.

Chapter 10: Grooming the Japanese Bobtail

In addition, you need to watch for mats and other tangles that can get in the cat's coat. This is especially the case if you have a Japanese Bobtail with a longer coat. You might want to use a small bit of water on any mats or snags and then separate them by hand before brushing. This is to ensure that you can actually get your cat's hair to be brushed out quite well.

6) How to Brush the Fur of Your Japanese Bobtail

Brushing may seem like a very ordinary task. It might seem trivial when you think about the coat of your Japanese Bobtail too. However, if done right, the benefits of brushing your Japanese Bobtail cat will be multiplied. If you look up any blog or book with Japanese Bobtail cat information then you will see that brushing is suggested as a great grooming technique. Here is how you can brush the fur of your cat the 'right' way.

Use the brush that you have for the cat by giving strokes from the head to tail of the cat and remove any loose, dead hairs. Take particular care while brushing the area under the cat's armpits, as the skin here is very fine and sensitive. Do not use scissors to cut any hair knots or mats.

You can get your Japanese Bobtail brushed off with a slick, short-bristled brush that has steel bristles. These brushes not only keep the fur neat but they can also massage the skin of your cat. All types of cats, especially the Japanese Bobtail, love this type of brushing action. The shorter bristles will make it so the hair will be treated well while you'll have an easier time with taking care of the brushing process.

Make sure all the strokes are even and in the direction of the fur. This will help eliminate the loose hairs and actually massage the cat's body.

Using a cat hairbrush, brush off all the loose hairs from your cat's body.

Chapter 10: Grooming the Japanese Bobtail

You can even use your grooming gloves to get rid of any debris that is visible on your cat's coat.

Your cat's skin consists of several natural oils. Massaging the body thoroughly after brushing will help distribute this oil evenly across the cat's body to produce healthier and shiner fur.

Make sure the bristles of the brush are not too sharp so the cat will not feel irritated while combing its fur. You must also ensure that you do not apply too much pressure while brushing the fur. It can cause cuts and bruises. This is especially critical when you consider the way that the brush will get closer to the skin, what with the coat being short.

7) Trimming the Nails of the Japanese Bobtail cat

It is best to trim your cat's nails once a week; you can do it every five to seven days for the best results. The key is to keep the cat from feeling irritated or experiencing too many pains while walking. A cat that has longer nails will not feel all that comfortable when walking.

Several tools can be used to trim the nails of the cat. You can easily use a cat nail cutter to trim the nails of the cat; this is because a human nail cutter may not be all that safe for your cat to manage. There is specialized equipment also available for the trimming of animal's nails such as a nail guillotine. Just ensure that the tool is reasonably sharp.

You need to keep the tool sharp because it will be strong to use. A dull edge can crash the nails of the cat. The goal is to just trim the fine edges of the nails of the cat. Just ensure that there is enough light when you are performing the trimming of the cat's nails. This makes sure that the tool is used just at the intended portions and does not damage the whole nail or skin of the cat, which can get fatal due to bleeding.

A nail trimmer is the cheapest grooming tool that you can get for your cat. It will cost you under $10 or £6 in most cases. This is a

Chapter 10: Grooming the Japanese Bobtail

very simple tool to use. The reason most cat owners make use of these nail clippers is to ensure that the upholstery and furniture in the house is protected from the sharp claws of the cat.

There are several types of clippers that are available on the market. The safest ones are the cat claw scissors that come with blunt ends to protect the cat from cuts and clipping injuries.

Many pet owners think of declawing as a suitable grooming technique. This surgical procedure removes the claws of the cat entirely. Also known as an onychectomy, this procedure involves the removal of the end bones of the cat's toes. The entire portions of the bone will typically be removed in the process.

This practice is very common in North America. However, because of the effects it has on the cat and its wellbeing, it is also considered animal cruelty in many parts of the world. This is due to how a good part of the cat's bone structure can be substantially impacted as a result of the practice.

This practice is followed in order to prevent the cat from damaging furniture and property. Other pet owners also justify declawing a cat as a method of protecting other people from being scratched or hurt by their cat. In many apartments, people are not allowed to keep cats unless they are completely declawed.

It is quite certain that these people do not understand the seriousness of this procedure. It is not a way of keeping the nails trimmed or blunt. Medical surgery has untoward repercussions on the cat. The toenails of your cat are actually attached very closely to its bones.

Therefore, removing the claw is as good as amputating the toes of your cat. The period of recovery is extremely painful for the cat. There is also no guarantee that your beloved pet will recover entirely from this traumatic experience. For this reason, several European countries have strong laws against declawing cats.

Chapter 10: Grooming the Japanese Bobtail

The Japanese Bobtail cat is very peaceful and pleasant by nature. With declawing, however, several owners swear by the fact that the personality of the cat changes. There are valid reasons to support this change in behavior and personality of the cat.

The biting frequency and strength increases in most cats. The only possible explanation for this is that when a cat loses one form of defense, it activates another.

House soiling is twice as common in declawed cats. Firstly, they become reluctant to walk and put pressure on their paws. In addition to that, severe cases like nerve dysfunction and even lameness renders the cat quite helpless.

Aggression is very common in cats post declawing. The pain makes them more defensive against people. In addition, the fact that you as the owner inflicted that pain upon it makes you less trustworthy in the eyes of the cat.

Almost 45% of cats that have been declawed are referred to vet teaching hospitals and cat schools to sort out behavioral issues. The change in behavior is more drastic if the cat has undergone tendonectomy in the process of being declawed. The repercussions of these behavior changes include relinquishing cats to shelters. For a cat like the Japanese Bobtail, which is so attached to people, this experience is extremely traumatic and can keep that cat from trusting in other people. Therefore, it is best for you to avoid trying to declaw your Japanese Bobtail when looking for ways to take care of the pet.

8) Dental Care

Dental care is very important for cats. It is almost as important as it is in humans. The truth is that cats tend to have huge amounts of tartar deposits on their teeth. This may result in gum damage and even tooth decay. Instead of taking your pet to the vet for cleaning procedures, you can simply keep a brushing kit to keep your cat's teeth in the best condition possible. If you do not maintain your cat's dental health, chances are that you will end up spending close to $500 or £300 on the anesthesia, antibiotics and other medicines required.

You will need to brush your cat's teeth regularly. You can get your cat used to having it's teeth brushed by first inserting your hands into its mouth, before using the toothbrush. Move it around as you would a toothbrush until the cat feels comfortable. Only then can you use the toothbrush to clean its teeth. You can buy pet toothpaste from most pet stores or vets, but please do not use human toothpaste.

Make sure you brush your cat's teeth two or three times in a week. This is to allow the teeth to feel healthy. In addition, make sure you start doing this when your cat is at an early age so the cat will feel more comfortable with what you are trying to do with it.

9) Eye Care for the Japanese Bobtail cat

If you think that your Japanese Bobtail has excessive tear staining then it is better to consult your veterinary doctor. In case they are reasonably short and have no medical conditions then you can also use any of the commercial eye stain removal products for cats yourself. However, excretions from the eyes are generally signs of unhealthy eyes, so always consult a vet.

10) Ear Care of the Japanese Bobtail cat

The ears are also a pivotal organ of cats and should be given the utmost care for health and hygienic reasons. It is especially important to consider this for the Japanese Bobtail, as this cat tends to have more hair around the ears than most other cats. It doesn't take much for some ear mites and other annoying problems to get in the way of the ears.

The attendant or the master should inspect the ears of the Japanese Bobtail cat every week. Unattended ears can result in the development of ear-mites, bacterial infections, allergies and yeast infections inside the ears. Regular inspection and the cleaning of the ears can make sure that the cat is safe from such allergies and infections.

You can always consider trimming the ears with a special pair of ear trimming scissors. These should only be used if the cat is very calm and relaxed.

It helps to use a cotton swab with a non-oily ear cleaner that does not contain alcohol around the outer parts of the ear. Work upward from the canal and never go deep into the ear while working on this process. This can help you to clear out old stains. You can also rinse the ears out after you are done with this process; be sure to again go outward from the ears.

Redness inside the ear can be the main sign of infection. If such is the case then it is highly advised to consult your veterinary doctor in order to prevent any other defect or reaction. Begin the cleaning process of the cat's ears by using ear cleanser or a medicated ear wipe. Such equipment can be easily purchased either from a veterinary doctor clinic or from a pet store. Properly rinse the ear with water after applying the cleanser or the medicated wipe and thoroughly dry it after this is done.

11) Bathing the Japanese Bobtail cat

Like with any other cat breed, it helps to bathe the Japanese Bobtail every once in a while. It's true that such a cat will know how to clean itself if its mother trains it properly. However, the coat will need to be bathed when the cat gets into a really messy situation. This is also important for cases when the cat has fleas or other pests that have to be brushed off.

You can begin the bathing session by using special kitty shampoo that is readily available at most veterinary shops. Make sure that the shampoo is suitable for your cat by reading the instructions. Do not ever use any shampoo that is meant for dogs or any other animal, as it can cause serious itchy conditions to the cat and can

Chapter 10: Grooming the Japanese Bobtail

damage the coat of the cat. If necessary, dilute the shampoo with some water. You can also use a special cat conditioner, which will give a healthy and shiny finish to the coat of the cat's body. Use a washcloth to spread and massage the shampoo throughout the body of the cat.

You clearly have to use a light amount of shampoo on the cat. This is to keep from having far too many suds.

Avoid shampoo going in the eyes of the cat as it can cause the eyes to itch. Once the massaging is done, put the cat in a tub filled with water. Just ensure that the head of the cat stays out. Rinse out the shampoo thoroughly by using the shower or using a bath mug all over the body of the cat. After you make sure that all the shampoo is rinsed out, then take a wet cloth and gently rub it all over the cat's body. This will help in removing the loose, dead hairs from the body of the cat.

Then you need to have a dry towel ready. Use it all over the cat's body to thoroughly dry its coat. After this, you are all done with bathing your cat. Hopefully, your Japanese Bobtail cat would come out very nice, clean and shiny from the bathroom.

This is needed to provide the cat with a better look. It will maintain the beautiful white color of the cat's fur and will be easy for the cat to bear with thanks to how well it may be managed.

Chapter 11: Feeding the Japanese Bobtail

1) Nutrition

Nutrition is essential in all cats, especially in terms of energy. The Japanese Bobtail needs to obtain important substances for energy production or for maintaining the body's metabolic process.

The vet can give you instructions on the important and necessary nutrients that could help your Japanese Bobtail cat. The cat may get the nutrients from quality commercial feeds sold in shops; these are processed to meet various nutritional standards. There are various nutrients that are essential for your cat.

A good standard is to think about how much food the cat needs. A Bobtail should eat about 35 calories for every pound that the cat weighs. This should be good enough to take care of the requirements that the cat has for a healthy and safe diet.

These cats are closely related to fiercer felines like lions and tigers. These Bobtail cats do not eat everything; it means they are inflexible and as an owner, you must know that. You cannot feed them everything as we do for dogs and other domestic species. Japanese Bobtail cats do not process excess of carbohydrates as dogs do and these high carbs can damage their digestive systems.

You'll have to see if your cat is willing to take in whatever food you are trying to offer. First, try to feed your cat with a taste test. If it likes to eat that thing, offer it with plenty of food but try to take some guidelines from an experienced doctor because cats like a little moisture and fresh food. The other thing is that you may offer your cat with plenty of one dietary nutrient and there will occur a deficiency of other nutrients.

As mentioned earlier, 35 calories per pound is important for the diet but fortunately for you, it should not be all that hard to manage. This is needed considering how active the cat can be; it needs these extra calories in order to maintain its energy as well as possible. Still, as human beings need carbohydrates, protein, and vitamins, cats also need them but in different proportions.

Scientists have found that different species of cats have different nutritional requirements but if you are more serious about their health then you must have to take into account the age, sex, species, and health of the cat. Kittens need more energy to grow and as they mature they need less energy to keep them active and healthy.

Vitamins and minerals are also necessary for these cats because they enhance the catalyst reactions and make the cat more attractive, energetic, and smart. Regarding minerals, these should be provided in the diet because animals do not metabolize minerals if they are provided separately. Beet pulp is mostly used in cat feed because it promotes a healthy gut and avoids undesirable side effects.

Vitamin supplements are not suggested for your cat because cats do not digest these as well as people can. Still, you can give them out only when a veterinarian diagnosed a mineral deficiency in the cat.

Regarding nutrients, you should consult a nutritionist and can follow nutritional tables provided by the doctors. In case of malnutrition, use a healthy and clean diet for your Japanese Bobtail so the cat will have a healthy lifestyle without being at risk of serious problems over a period of time.

2) Water

To all living beings, water is very essential to the body. In the Japanese Bobtail cat, the water content comprises about 60 to 70 percent of the total body weight, meaning water plays a major role. The food that the pet takes is either dry foods, which consist

Chapter 11: Feeding the Japanese Bobtail

of about 10 percent of moisture and also canned food, which has a total percentage of 78% moisture.

This means that for good health, the pet should at least have enough water available in the body. If the pet loses about 10 percent of water, it can lead to serious consequences, which lead to a decrease in weight and other health complications. Water is also essential in the digestive process. Water is used to soften hard foods during the food breakdown in the stomach.

3) Proteins

Proteins are essential. They are the building blocks of cells, tissues, organs, and enzymes. Let us start by discussing what the essential amino acids are. Essential amino acids are the acids in proteins that cannot be broken by the pet in enough quantities. Animal experts insist that such kinds of amino acids must be provided in the diet. These amino acids include:

- Arginine
- Methionine
- Histidine
- Threonine
- Leucine
- Tryptophan
- Taurine

The essential amino acid known as taurine is crucial in the prevention of diseases and helps in reproduction and growth. These kinds of amino acids also help in the sight of the pet. The amino acids can be found easily from eggs, meat and fish.

Non-essential amino acids are important despite their low concentration in amino acids. The proteins obtained from the

Chapter 11: Feeding the Japanese Bobtail

vegetables can be easily broken down by the pet. The amino acids are found also in cereals and soy. They contain a minimal concentration of glucose, fats and amino acids. They are not found in the diet.

4) Fats

Experts say that fats provide essential energy in bulk. If you wish to provide your pet with the much-needed energy, then fats can provide up to two times more energy than even proteins and carbohydrates. The fats in the body could be used in the production of cells, repairing those that have been wounded and play a major role in the productions of hormones within the body of the cat.

The fatty acids just like the essential amino acids in proteins can only be given to the pet in the diet. The fats are vital in the absorption of fat-soluble vitamins and the fats protect the inner organs of the pet. The cat cannot be given the fats in any other form other than through diet, this is because the pet will be able to synthesize the fats in the diet. In the breakdown of these fats, water is important.

A slight deficiency in fats could mean skin problems to the pet and a decrease in the total weight of the animal. An acid known as Arachidonic, which is an omega-6 fatty acid, is one of the acids that plays a great role in maintaining the skin and coat of the Japanese Bobtail. The acid also plays an important role during reproduction and the kidney functionality of the pet.

Omega-6 and omega-3 fatty acids have an equally essential role in the pet. Both of these fatty acids, which are found in fats, help to heal inflammation. The experts who have experience in the nutrition of the Bobtail say that if the omega-6 can be replaced by omega-3, then the fatty acids could help with various parts of the pet. It can help in making skin problems less likely to occur.

Chapter 11: Feeding the Japanese Bobtail

Arthritis, which is a joint disease, can be rectified using the fatty acids present in fats. Bowel disease can also be healed. An important note here is that if you give the Japanese Bobtail homemade fats, it will be difficult for you to know or measure the amount of fats you give it.

5) Carbohydrates

Carbohydrates are also energy giving nutrients, which are important to the pet. The carbohydrates are vital and important in the intestinal health of the Japanese Bobtail. The nutrients are also important in the reproduction process. Diarrhea can be tamed in the small intestine by fibers in carbohydrates that are modified to mix bacterial populace.

If the Japanese Bobtail is to benefit from the fiber found in carbohydrates then those carbs must be in a simpler form for the body to easily absorb them. These fibers must be fermentable. Low fermentable sources lead to poor development and less surface for the intestinal mucosa.

Excess mucus and flatulence is a course of high production of gases and by-products of high fermentable fibers in carbohydrates. Moderate fibers can be easily gotten from beet pulp and they are best known for the promotion of a healthy gut. Other examples of fiber can include corn, wheat and rice.

An important caution is that these fibers are high in energy levels and that is why the experts do not recommend high-energy carbohydrate concentrated foods to younger and growing Japanese Bobtail. The experts say there is no minimum set amount of carbohydrate requirement for the Bobtail; there must be a limitation on the level of glucose that the pet is given.

6) Vitamins

Vitamins are catalysts for enzymes in the pet. The Japanese Bobtail needs vitamins to catalyze enzymes, keeping in mind the large amount of the vitamins required, they could not be synthesized in the body, hence they are given in the diet. Giving a vitamin supplement is not a wise thing to do on a Japanese Bobtail; it is deemed unnecessary unless the veterinary expert recommends the supplement vitamin in order to counter a disease or a particular disorder.

Due to more supplement vitamin practice in the recent days, which is commonly known as hypervitaminosis, it has turned to be poisonous. Excess vitamin A may lead to disorders in the pet. The excess of such a vitamin causes pain in the joints, brittle bones and dry skin. An excess total of vitamin D is not healthy for the Japanese Bobtail as it may cause bone calcification and pain in the joints. Tiny amounts of vitamins are very essential for the metabolic process in the pet. It is also important to note that vitamins play a key role in catalyzing enzymes that provide the body with energy.

7) Minerals

These nutrients also play a key role in terms of the bodily metabolic process, bone formation, strength and to maintain the fluid balance within the body. Minerals do not give out energy and they are not metabolized at all. The minerals constitute much of the bone structure and they are crucial to the overall health of the cat. In general, minerals are nutrients that the pet's body need for growth and survival. The cat cannot synthesize these nutrients, hence they are only given in the diet. Cats are very sensitive and you should take care of their diet because like dogs they can't digest everything and odd feeding behaviors alter the whole metabolism.

8) A Word About Milk

Milk can be useful for younger cats that are less than a year in age but you need to be extremely careful when using it. The fact is that milk is not healthy for an adult cat. Cats are able to tolerate and digest milk only when they are kittens. In adult cats, the digestive system is unable to process dairy products and, therefore, health issues like diarrhea and other digestive issues become quite common.

9) Give your cat a low fat diet

The Japanese Bobtail is quite an active cat by nature. Unfortunately, if it becomes obese or overweight, you will notice an evident reduction in its activity levels. For an indoor cat, which is not very active, a low fat diet is mandatory.

If you have put your cat on a weight loss diet, you must give him/her adequate amounts of protein. It is true that the calorie intake must be restricted. However, you must always make sure that you do not reduce the amount of essential nutrients. When you increase the amount of proteins, weight loss is aided while keeping the lean body mass intact.

10) Keep a check on the treats

If you are concerned about the health of your cat, make sure you reduce the amount of treats and tidbits. This practice must be extended to at least a couple of weeks after the 'diet' period. You must make sure that everyone in your family is aware of this rule.

If you try and cheat out of affection, remember that you are harming your cat's health. It would help, instead, to cut your cat's meal down to smaller, more frequent meals. This will ensure that he/she does not experience hunger pangs while continuing to stay on a healthy diet.

11) Say no to crash diets

Crash diets are harmful for cats just as they are harmful for humans. You must never starve your cat. In fact, no matter what restrictions you make in his/her diet, a dietician must supervise it. If you do not keep tabs on the amount of minerals and vitamins your cat is getting, it can lead to a fatal condition called hepatic lipidosis, which affects the liver.

12) Keep the activity levels high

Exercise is extremely important in cats. You cannot control the health and weight of your cat by merely altering the diet. You must ensure that he/she has an active lifestyle. While controlling the calories it takes in, you must also make sure that it burns the calories through exercise and activity. Here are some things you must do to make your cat's environment stimulating and engaging:

Set aside a dedicated time to play with your cat. You can use simple toys like strings to help your kitty play and get a good workout.

Allow its natural instincts to take over. You must let your cat climb, scratch and even chase around the house. These exercises are interesting to him/her, by nature, and will increase the process of weight loss. The Japanese Bobtail does particularly well with hunting activities and will really love pouncing on items and going after them as desired.

Get a feeding ball to give your cat for one meal in the day. The advantage with the feeding ball is that your cat will have to put in some amount of effort to roll the ball and get to the food inside.

The food bowl of your cat can be placed on top of a flight of stairs. This will encourage him/her to climb to get to the food.

Try to take your cat outdoors as often as possible. A breath of fresh air will do you and your kitty a great deal of good. Of course, you should be careful when making it work as keeping your cat outdoors for too long could be dangerous considering the conditions that your cat might get into.

Throughout the process of weight loss, you must be extremely patient. It will take several weeks and even months for your cat to

Chapter 11: Feeding the Japanese Bobtail

lose weight. If you find it too hard to maintain the weight of your cat on your own, you can ask your vet for tips. You can even enroll in a veterinary weight loss clinic for additional support and information.

Cats do not always like things that human beings like. Here we are going to talk about the human graded sushi that is liked by many of us but for cats, it is very dangerous. In raw fish, there is an enzyme called thiamine, which breaks down an essential vitamin "B" in cats. Deficiency of thiamine causes serious neurological conditions in cats.

Onions and chives cause anemia in felines. Don't feed raw onions to your cat because it will break down red blood cells due to toxic alliums present in onions. Traces of this diet might be used and if they are offered in cooked form then it is a safe diet.

A Japanese Bobtail cat should not be fed eggs at any time. We all know that eggs are the best source of protein but uncooked eggs are more prone to salmonella and they might cause a disease called "pancreatitis" in cats. It is an inflammation of the pancreas and leads to severe cases. Eggs can be occasionally fed to cats.

We often feed bones to cats but they are not the right source of energy for them. Bones cause perforation of the intestine and choking in cats. In addition, bones are hard and cat's teeth are not shaped to crush these bones. Hard bones cause teeth fractures in different species of cats.

Although some vets may recommend dry foods for Japanese Bobtail cats, it is important to note that there are many health defects that can be caused by such a food as this. It is also possible that the clinic and the curriculum of the veterinary clinic are funded by these pet food companies, making it mandatory for them to recommend dry kibble as a suitable option for your cat's diet. However, the truth is that the nutritional benefits of dry kibble are a lot less than the wet, canned foods.

Chapter 11: Feeding the Japanese Bobtail

If you try to save a few hundred dollars on your cat food, remember that you will end up paying several hundred dollars in helping your cat recover from nutrition related issues. Remember that your cat food must be a good source of protein. If you are unable to do that, he/she will be malnourished and unhealthy.

Cheaper varieties of cat food will only be able to provide your cat with plant-based proteins. For an animal that is an obligate carnivore, the only good source of protein is animal protein. In addition to this, these cheap foods also contain high amounts of carbohydrates that can make your cat obese or diabetic. Make sure you only bring home high quality foods for your pet.

According to the requirements, your Japanese Bobtail cat needs only a few hundred calories a day. You can offer cheese but in very little amounts. Try not to feed your cat a human diet because it causes digestive problems and human vitamin supplements damage the inner lining of the feline's digestive tract. The kidneys and liver are also damaged by feeding your cat a human dietary supplement.

Try to contact a veterinarian urgently in case of food poisoning because cats are very sensitive and can't bear serious health problems. If you are consulting feeding charts and feed them a specialized diet then you are the lucky one to have a healthy, smart, and active cat.

13) Foods you must never give your cat

The kinds of foods that your cat eats and you eat are extremely different from each other. The entire digestive ability is quite different and hence, the food should also be significantly different.

Many pet owners make the mistake of giving their cats the same food that is cooked in their home. Now, let's put it this way, do you think of dry kibble or canned fish as an appropriate food for

Chapter 11: Feeding the Japanese Bobtail

you? Well, then how do you expect your cat to fulfill its nutritional requirements with the foods that you eat?

Usually pet owners think that their little beauties are sure of what is best for them. Cats are known to be picky eaters but there is little evidence that suggests that a cat knows what is right for it and what is wrong. Perhaps in the wild, cats follow their instincts and get the right nutrition. However, with domesticated cats, the varieties of foods that are available to them will make them reach out for all the wrong goodies. Not only are these foods nutritionally poor, they can also be quite dangerous for your cat. As we mentioned earlier, it is very easy to feed your cat the wrong things. They will enjoy just about anything that you feed them. In addition, in the assumption that your cat is happy, you will continue to give him/her food that can causes serious health related issues. Here are some foods that are a complete no-no for your beloved pet:

Tuna
Although this does sound strange, there is a good chance that your cat will get addicted to tuna. Of course a share of tuna now and then should not harm your cat too much. However, a steady tuna diet can cause malnutrition in your cat. Although cats savor tuna and really enjoy it, the nutrients available are not too many. Another common issue with tuna is mercury poisoning. Never keep open tuna cans within the reach of your cat. You can serve it occasionally but make sure that it knows that it is not available all the time.

Chives, Garlic, Onion
These are common ingredients in all our foods but they have disastrous health impacts on cats. Any form of these vegetables, cooked, powdered or even raw can cause anemia in cats by completely breaking down their red blood cells. Even though human baby food consists of powdered onion, do not consider it safe for your kitty. Onion poisoning and even gastrointestinal problems might arise if your cat eats chives, garlic or onion.

Chapter 11: Feeding the Japanese Bobtail

Alcohol
Your cat must never ever consume any form of alcohol. Make sure that all the liquor in your home is out of your cat's reach. The effects on the cats' liver and brain are similar to the effects on the human brain. In cats, however, the amount of alcohol required to do this damage is a lot lesser. A 5-pound cat can go into a coma with just two teaspoons of liquor. Even one teaspoon more can be fatal for your kitty.

Raisins and Grapes
Many cat owners consider grapes and raisins as suitable treats for their cats. This is never a good idea. Giving your cat too many raisins or grapes can also lead to kidney failure eventually. Even a small share of grapes can really make your cat fall sick. Vomiting is one early sign of illness caused by grapes. Some cats may have no reactions but we are not sure of the long-term effects of feeding grapes to your cat.

Caffeine
An overdose of caffeine can actually kill your cat. With caffeine intake, there is no antidote either. The most common symptoms of caffeine poisoning in cats include restlessness, fast-paced breathing, heart palpitations and muscle tremors.

Caffeine is not only found in coffee. There are several other sources including beans, chocolates, colas and even energy drinks. Some medicines and painkillers also contain substantial amounts of caffeine.

Chocolate
It is impossible to say no to your adorable cat staring at you while you gorge on chocolate. However, this treat can end up being extremely harmful for your little pet. Chocolate consists of a toxic material known as theobromine. This is extremely dangerous for cats. It is found in all forms of chocolate including white chocolate. The common problems associated with chocolate are muscle tremors, seizures, heart changes and even death.

Chapter 11: Feeding the Japanese Bobtail

Candy
Any sweetened food including candy, gum, toothpaste and baked goods contain an element called xylitol. This element can pace up the circulation of insulin in the cat's body. As a result, the level of sugar in the cat's body drops suddenly, causing seizures and liver failure in your cat.

Bones and Fat Trimmings
Scraps from the table are fed so often to cats but they may cause serious health disorders in cats. Fat, whether cooked or uncooked, can result in vomiting, diarrhea and intestinal problems in your cat. If a cat chokes on a bone, it can be fatal. Other problems related to the bones are lacerations and obstructions due to the splinters.

Raw Eggs
Many people believe that raw eggs are a healthy dietary option for their cat. However, this is not true. There are two primary health issues that result from consumption of raw eggs. Firstly, food poisoning may occur due to the presence of bacteria like E coli. Secondly, a certain protein in the egg white, known as avidin, can reduce the absorption of vitamin B in cats, leading to skin related issues.

Raw Meat
Although many of you may argue that cats only eat raw meats in the wild, the truth is that uncooked meat and fish can be harmful to cats. They contain bacteria and microorganisms that might cause food poisoning. Additionally, certain enzymes present in raw fish can destroy essential vitamins like thiamine in the cat's body. This can cause neurological problems and can also result in a coma in extreme cases.

Dog Food
A bite once in a while will not harm your cat too much. However, the formula used in dog food is definitely not suitable for cats. Cat food is packed with necessary proteins and vitamins that can

help the cat fulfill its nutritional requirements. On the other hand, dog foods can also contain plant proteins that are not suitable for your cat. If your cat regularly consumes dog food, it might become malnourished.

Liver
Giving your cat liver once in a while is not an issue. However, too much liver can lead to vitamin A toxicity in cats. This is a serious condition as it affects the bones. There might be deformities and also bone growths and spurts on the spine. Osteoporosis can also be observed in cats with vitamin A toxicity. It can be rather fatal in the most extreme cases.

Yeast Dough
Uncooked dough is never recommended for a cat. If the cat consumes it, there are chances that the dough will actually raise inside the cat's stomach. During this expansion, the dough may stretch the abdomen in the cat and also cause alcohol poisoning as the yeast ferments.

Being cautious sometimes isn't good enough. Your cat might just make its way into your pantry and have a generous helping of restricted foods. There is no need to be alarmed. In most cases, your vet will be able to provide an antidote to take care of the situation for you.

Chapter 12: Travelling with your Japanese Bobtail

Sadly, cats are not the best travel companions. If you have had a dog for a pet, never assume that your Japanese Bobtail will be as easy to travel with as anyone else you might want to head out on the road with. Cats are extremely fussy travelers and you must take utmost care to ensure that they do not feel too distressed when you are taking them out for a considerably long ride.

The Japanese Bobtail may be a good cat when it comes to travelling but it is always a challenge to predict what your cat will do. Sometimes your cat might feel really sick while travelling. In other cases your cat will be fine.

You might want to talk with a breeder that you are getting your Japanese Bobtail from about whether or not the cat is capable of travelling well. This includes asking if the cat is comfortable with travel and if that pet is irritated by motion. This is to give you a better idea of whether or not that cat will be comfortable or safe for travel purposes.

1) Travelling by car

Remember that you must never leave the cat open in the car. If your cat decides to pounce on the driver, the repercussions could be fatal. Make sure that you always carry your cat in a carrier. The carrier should be extremely sturdy and must be made from metallic wires or even fiberglass. The carriers made from light plastic or even cardboard are not meant for long journeys. They are only suitable for short trips like a visit to the vet.

The weather that you travel in is extremely important in deciding what measures you need to take while travelling, if you think that it will get hotter as you proceed, make sure that you get a carrier

Chapter 12: Travelling with your Japanese Bobtail

that allows a good amount of air circulation. In case it is going to get cold along the way, carry enough blankets to wrap your cat up and keep him/her warm.

There are also draft free carriers that will ensure that you do not leave your kitty shivering and uncomfortable. Irrespective of the kind of carrier that you buy, there is one more thing that you need to consider. In case you are planning on changing your mode of transport along the way, plane for example, you must also check for the guidelines that they provide with respect to the type of carrier that is allowed.

If you have ample space in the back of your car and you only intend to travel by car, you can even use a large crate to keep your cat in. All you need to do is place blankets and sheets inside this crate and put it in the back of your car. The only thing that you need to ensure is that you provide your cat with a quiet place where he/she can rest during the journey. Place his/her favorite toys and treats around him/her to reduce the stress of travelling. The bedding that you provide during the travelling period should be one that he/she is already used to.

Make sure the crate or the carrier is completely secure. Even if you were to apply the brakes suddenly, it must be safe. If the carrier or crate falls suddenly, your cat will be startled. The last thing you want while travelling is an anxious cat. If you are driving in a hatchback, never allow the cat to be placed in the boot, as this area is very dark and badly ventilated. Check on your cat regularly and make sure that he/she is comfortable.

Remember to make the carrier so it will be large enough for the cat to roam in. Anything that allows the cat to lie down without obstructions or to turn from one angle to the next will certainly help as it will keep your kitty from feeling overly contained or uncomfortable while in the carrier.

Chapter 12: Travelling with your Japanese Bobtail

2) Travelling by train

When you are travelling by train, you must obviously place your cat in a carrier. Since there are several other strangers on a train, you do not want to have any instances of your cat breaking free and scaring them.

So, make sure that the carrier that you have is extremely sturdy. The base of the carrier must be extremely strong to ensure that your cat is secured. The carrier must be light so that you do not have any difficulty carrying it around. It must also be of a convenient size depending upon the space available on the train. Make sure that you get a carrier that is large enough for your cat to rest in. Never cram your kitty into a small carrier because there isn't enough storage space.

You must keep a familiar blanket in the carrier to reduce anxiety. However, littering and soiling can be quite a concern. So, line your cat's cage with a good amount of absorbent paper so that you may both have a pleasant journey.

3) Travelling by air

Travelling with your pet by air requires a good deal of planning in advance. The airlines that you choose will also depend upon their efficiency in handling and transferring your cat. Most airlines will not allow the carrier into the cabin area. You may have to let your pet travel alone in a special section on the aircraft that is reserved for pets.

Cats will have very little trouble travelling by air. If you have a pregnant cat or a kitten less than three months of age travelling with you, it might become a matter of concern. It is recommended that you avoid air travel for these two categories of cats.

Check for a license to transport animals in the airlines that you choose. Chances are that you and your cat will travel by separate

Chapter 12: Travelling with your Japanese Bobtail

flights. If this is true, make sure that you get a direct flight for your cat so that he/she does not have to deal with issues like transits and transfers.

Be sure to talk with an airline about what you can do as well. If you can stay as open as possible about what you want to do then it should be rather easy for you to have a good outing.

Travelling with your Japanese Bobtail can be fun if you prepare him/her in advance. The most important thing to do is to condition it to enjoy sitting inside the carrier. If you are able to accomplish this, you have already won half the battle.

Chapter 13: Caring for the Japanese Bobtail

Chapter 13: Caring for the Japanese Bobtail

Health is a very important aspect of the Japanese Bobtail's life. Though once in a while along the way illness is inevitable, something of the utmost importance is how you deal with it. Cats such as the Japanese Bobtail are no exceptions since they are animals too and just like our everyday pals, or kids, they have to be cared for to remain healthy.

Simple yet complicated like any other animal care, this cat's health is equally wide and ranges from averting simple illnesses to just being fine and maintaining its fitness. A well cared for cat is therefore a role model of how cheap, and easy, living with a cat can be.

1) Signs and symptoms of illness

Come to think of it, doesn't caring for that Japanese Bobtail cat just give you joy when you see it purring and bouncing around with mirth all day long? Of course it does, however you must have a very keen eye for health and a perfect relationship with your cat to be able to tell whether it's healthy, ill, or just pulling your leg for a little groom. As the primary care giver to the cat, you should understand that it's your core duty to pay attention to your cat and always be there for it.

If illness knocks however, you should be aware that different pets will exhibit sickness symptoms differently and so shall the Japanese Bobtail cat. These signs and symptoms will vary in greater lengths but will still be evidently vivid if you pay close attention to the cat. Therefore, a clear sense of knowledge of these symptoms will prove to be very important since it will help you to get to your vet on time in any case sickness strikes. With a robust ability to notice any slight change, the cat's sickness will never get you off guard.

Chapter 13: Caring for the Japanese Bobtail

a. Strange Behavior

Your cat will rarely show signs of any strange behavior unless something is wrong. When the strong and fond Japanese Bobtail starts to display simple, questionable behavior, it might just be a sign of an imminent illness disaster and therefore care has to be taken. You should therefore start keeping it in sight.

Behaviors such as frequent visits to the litter box will be a very open factor to raise eyebrows. While most cats will tend to visit their litter boxes twice a day, some might just do so as often as the meals come in.

Yet in cases where your cat goes to urinate or defecate more than its normal rate, be weary that you might be on your way to the vet pretty soon. It is therefore prudent to always take a closer peep to your cat's litter box before you change or clean it to see if you can spot anything strange in it like traces of blood in the urine. This is because with such visible signs it is easy to tell if the cat is sick or not.

However, such behavior as acute loss of appetite are not signs to be brushed off so easily. If your cat stops to run after it's eating bowl, or just smells its favorite meal and walks away, and has not eaten in a whole day, something must be really wrong.

You should keep close tabs on your cat for at least 24 hours, you never know, there might just have been a cat party at the neighbor's yard. Cats at times also lose their mind due to mental disorders; although this might be hard to determine, be mindful of head tilting, dizziness, or disorientation. All these might be definite signs of neurological disorder, so in such cases, always be quick to do the right thing and visit the vet.

As we have seen before, a cat's personality is well defined. Unique only to every cat, it is no doubt its own way of telling who it is. Cats love to play, to exercise, and to run around all day long, but if lately your cat exhibits an exquisite form of tiredness or exhaustion, chances are its suffering from some deficiency syndromes. For example, lethargy and apathy are very great

Chapter 13: Caring for the Japanese Bobtail

symptoms of vitamin deficiency in these lovely creatures as previously seen.

It is well known that these cats are capable of swimming quite well. Still, this does not mean that they should be frequently found in the bathtubs or playing "hide and seek" in the kitchen sinks. Such constant behavior might just manifest the cat's frustration at something.

It might be trying to grab your attention for the wrong reasons. So maybe it's time to find out what's really bothering it, maybe walk it back to the vet, or just push it across its weighing scale. This way you may just be sure to note one or two abnormalities, since factors such as constant weight loss are direct pointers to deteriorating health.

You must understand that your cat also has mood swings and emotions that can go out of control. If you have observed a sudden change in the behavior of your Japanese Bobtail then you might want to be careful with that cat as the changes can be linked to emotional stress.

b. Symptoms of Stress

With a well-behaved cat like the Japanese Bobtail, it is very easy to notice the symptoms of stress. The most common symptoms include:

Loss of appetite

Reduced interaction with the members in the family

Aggressive behavior

Confinement to hiding places

Elimination out of the litter box

Too much grooming

Change in interaction with other pets in the house

It is possible that your cat displays more symptoms of stress, including a change in voice. It is impossible to compare the symptoms seen in two different cats. The intensity of the symptoms varies from one cat to another.

While in some cats the change is very drastic, some of them show such gradual progression that it is very easy to ignore. The Japanese Bobtail cat loves to interact with others. So, you must always be alert to behavior patterns like excessive hiding to make sure that you do not allow the emotional distress in your cat to escalate.

2) What Causes Stress in These Cats?

There are several causes for stress in cats. Now, there are some factors that we do not even consider potent enough to cause dramatic changes in the cat's behavior. However, there are many changes in the immediate environment of the cat that seem too ordinary for us. However, the impact that it has on your pet can be extremely damaging. These normal and usually overlooked causal factors include:

Installation of new carpets

Loud Music

Change in the brand of litter

Dirty litter box

Inclusion of new furniture

Visitors

Repairs in the house

Barking of dogs

Appearance of strange cats or dogs around the house

Chapter 13: Caring for the Japanese Bobtail

Travel

Change in the brand of food

Then, there are some causal factors that are very evident, as they have emotionally damaging effects on human beings as well. These factors include:

Divorce

Death in the Family

Birth of baby

Illness in the Family

Abuse

Inclusion of another pet

Natural disasters

Injuries

Moving to a new home

Cats, as we have discussed in previous chapters, need to get used to the sights and smells around them in order to be comfortable. However, if you make sudden changes in your cat's environment, you can expect it to feel distressed. It is possible that over time, your cat will overcome these issues. If they persist, however, it is a good idea to consult an animal therapist. Even your regular veterinary doctor will be able to check your cat for emotional distress and provide you with necessary solutions.

3) How to Reduce Emotional Stress in Japanese Bobtails

When you see one or more of the signs mentioned above, the first thing you need to do is have your Japanese Bobtail cat examined

Chapter 13: Caring for the Japanese Bobtail

by a doctor. The reason for stress must be identified at the earliest. Although this is not easy, you can do a background check to come to suitable conclusions.

The triggers for stress in your cat are not always evident. However, if you are aware of how sensitive your cat is then you will be able to determine the most obvious causes for stress.

It is important for you to understand that the hearing and smelling abilities of your feline companion are far better than yours. Even the faintest sound or smell that is easily neglected by you is picked up by your cat quite easily. Scents from another cat, new smells inside the house like fresh paint, scents of new people etc. can be very stressful for your cat. So, if you are aware of any changes that have taken place around your cat's environment, you must include it in the list of suspected causes.

Here are some things that you can do to reduce stress in your cat:

Prepare your cat for any big change that is impending.

Have enough spaces in the house where your cat can rest or hide. If your cat does not want to be bothered, allow it to have a safe retreat.

The litter box must be kept pristine. Try to keep the entire set up appealing to your cat. The location of the litter box, the type of litter used and the number of boxes you include should be given a good amount of thought.

If there are several cats in your house and you notice tension and change in behavior amongst them, you need to make several modifications. You must make sure that every cat in your home feels completely secure in its environment.

If your cat is getting too much attention from kids and visitors, keep it away from them. Even if the other pets in your home are giving it unnecessary attention, you should provide your

Chapter 13: Caring for the Japanese Bobtail

cat with a space where it will be able to spend some time alone, in peace.

Make sure you spend enough time with your cat. You must engage in interactive sessions and play with your cat to give it confidence. This is the only way you can develop a positive relationship with your cat based on affection and trust.

Cats never appreciate change. So, try to make them minimal, especially with things that are associated with the cat directly, like food, litter box and even water bowl. Any change around your cat must be gradual to help it accommodate it.

Enrich your cat's environment. Cats can get bored very easily and must be constantly engaged. So, try to include toys, puzzles and even entertainment DVDs as part of your stimulation kit. You must always ensure that your cat is having fun.

Never leave the cat alone. If you are travelling, get someone to take care of your cat. Japanese Bobtail cats can especially get extremely distressed when they are away from their owners even for one day.

The interactions that you have with your cat are extremely important in its emotional wellbeing. If you do notice stress in your cat, there is no need to be alarmed. All you have to do is give him/her as much time and affection as you can to help it get back to his/her old, playful self.

Overall, never try to diagnose your cat. Though you may be its immediate friend, it is important to humbly recognize cat diagnosis as being far from your expertise. Just understand your cat and come to appreciate observation as the key to this bond. Most of all understand that a well fed, rested, and protected cat is likely to remain healthier for longer.

a. Physical Clues
Physical clues are another greater than life factor to consider. Generally, a physical outlook would be quite revealing to any

Chapter 13: Caring for the Japanese Bobtail

source of pain or illness that a person or an animal might be going through.

Discharge usually is the most conspicuous of the physical consideration. From excessive mucus in the nose, teary eyes, to bloody cuts or rough fur, it would be very easy to tell if your cat is unwell. However, frequent grooming of your cat may just as well give you an edge to easily detect these physical injuries and pain. Usually seen on the outer coat of your cat or by simply grooming your cat's fur, physical clues should still reveal volumes up to the well-hidden kidney stones disorders.

Cats love to be touched and touching is a universal way of sensing, no more than hearing or tasting. It is therefore advisable to constantly groom your cat for lumps. Lumps will often be noticed only by touching.

That is why touching would be a more viable way to do it. Just like their human counterparts, female cats for instance are prone to breast cancer and grooming would be the perfect way to find out if this underlying threat might be knocking at your favorite pet.

Some sicknesses however will allow your eyes to do a fantastic job for you. A sickness that causes the cat's pupils to be dilated falls squarely in this category. If your cat's eyes are dilated or if one pupil is more dilated than the other, it is no doubt that your cat should see its vet. In addition to this, respiratory problems will manifest themselves vividly if you are always in constant contact with your cat.

This works well with a combination of many other factors. For instance you walk into your apartment, and suddenly your cat that jumps on your lap has this whizzing sound in its breathing. What suddenly crosses your mind? A difficulty in breathing most definitely. The opposite is also true; when your cat breathes very fast, heavily, or weakly, something must be going a miss, so don't hesitate to pick up your phone and dial that number that you know best, the vet's.

Chapter 13: Caring for the Japanese Bobtail

Again that is not enough, as usually traits of sicknesses may run over and over again, but even in that recurrence those few that may stand out or generalize the rest, like discoloration of the cat's gums and unkempt coat, are the main factors that add strength to these content of physique. Black or very pale gums, together with paleness around the eyes and ears would specifically point to an ill cat.

Although a foul smell from the mouth might indicate the same, nothing is more crystal clear than unkempt fur or the loss of so much fur on the coat. The latter may depict stress due to change of environment or simply sickness and an urgent need to see a vet.

Sometimes your cat may act strangely with mucus, blood, and a discolored coat and this must be checked out. Consultation is the best medicine for these many diseases.

4) Examining for specific illnesses

Questions of whether your cat is going to be fine, or if it will make it through might just stress your mind, but with a rough idea you can always calmly take it to the vet with no hesitation of an end of the odds. With a little help you can always be able to relate your cat's symptoms to more specific illnesses and this way you are able to know what urgent measures to take.

Here are some specific illnesses:

a. Flea Infestation
Fleas are a very common source of infections to many domesticated animals; even the Japanese Bobtail that you are so fond of is not immune to them. Therefore, if you see your cat scratching often, do an immediate spot check by running a fine tooth comb through the coat while keeping an eye out for those tiny little black insects.

You can also lie them down on a sheet of white paper and see if any will fall off; if that is the case, ask your vet for the right medication. Fleas in most cases may act as a source of discomfort to your cat, and as if to add salt to the wound, they will make your kittens anemic, or worse transmit other infections such as *Ctenocephalides Felis* commonly known as the cat flea and which always carry worms with it.

b. Hairballs
Formed at the back of the throat or in the small intestines, hairballs will cause a bad smell in your cat's mouth. In extreme cases hairballs may become matted hair or cause undigested, foul-smelling food as feces or vomit, leading to an eventual surgery of your cat.

To solve this, ensure that you groom your cat often and give the cat a balanced diet to allow it to pass out the hairballs or just cough it out. Pumpkin pulp would add fiber to digest down the hairball and egg yolk would do just great in adding proteins that break down the hairball, therefore you may just consider adding these to your cat recipe and serving it with a balanced diet.

c. Overactive Thyroid and Constipation
Characterized by increased appetite, thirst or unexplained weight loss, an overactive thyroid will be a great source of weakness, nervousness, vomiting, lethargy, diarrhea, and messy coat. The best way to deal with is to see your vet and ensure the right medication for your cat.

With dry, hard stool, it is easy to tell if your cat is constipated. Cats get constipated due to many reasons, such as ingestion of foreign objects, enlarged prostate gland, dehydration, low fiber diet, or maybe the effects of specific medications. While the signs are so broad and confusion imminent, getting the right advice or medication is the best way to ensure that your Japanese Bobtail is safe.

d. Feline Diabetes
Also known as diabetes mellitus, this is common in almost all cat breeds. Feline diabetes includes increased urination (polyuria) vomiting, dehydration, weakness, loss of appetite, and increased

Chapter 13: Caring for the Japanese Bobtail

thirst (polydipsia). Breathing abnormalities and in most cases an unkempt coat will also accompany its symptoms and signs.

Although it may affect cats of all ages, it is more common with older cats 10 years old and above or obese male cats. The best way to find out is to take your cat for blood and urine sugar sampling, as this will assure you of a concrete medication and dependable results.

5) Medical Disorders

From the topic "examining for specific illnesses" we see how you can use different signs to find out if your Japanese Bobtail is ill or not and even add a few pointers to what they might be suffering from.

However, it doesn't show us what exactly they may be suffering from since medical disorders are so many, and while you are very much advised against diagnosing your own cat, it is of great advantage to know what the vet will be treating your cat for, and better still, it will feel easier if you just had a little knowledge prior to your meeting with the vet. This way you will be sure to ask relevant questions or even to have a better idea of the understanding what is required of you.

a. Feline Immunodeficiency Virus (FIV)
Belonging to the same group as Human Immunodeficiency Virus, this medical disorder belongs purely to cats. FIV with its slow viruses is known for its lifelong infections and slow progressive diseases.

b. Feline Leukemia Virus (FeLV)
This is a feline retrovirus that causes both cancerous and non-cancerous diseases. It is easily destroyed by detergents, warmth, and will not survive long outside your cat. Carried mostly in urine, tears, and feces of infected cats, it is not contagious, but only by a direct, prolonged, wet contact with the infected cats.

Chapter 13: Caring for the Japanese Bobtail

There is no evidence that FeLV would be transmittable to humans.

c. Cat Ringworm
The most common of all skin infections in domestic cats is a fungal infection spread through spores. This disorder may not bother your cat, since it is a self limiting disease and will come and go as it pleases, however treating it might also be difficult and the scars might be difficult to remove.

d. Feline Infectious Peritonitis (FIP)
The leading cause of cat deaths and the most feared disease of the domesticated cats, FIP has wiped out many cats. Caused by a corona virus infection, FIP has proven hard to diagnose, as most of its tests are never accurate. It is for this reason too that it has managed to lead to the deaths of many cats.

e. Feline Urinary Tract Disease
This is always a combination of different symptoms and may just be readily confused with other diseases. Diseases of the urinary tract occur mostly in cats affecting both males and females in greater numbers. They affect the bladder through the urethra. Sometimes it may lead to the obstruction of the urinary tract system and to eventual death. However, it has a better diagnosis, better symptoms, and so it's readily understood and well treated so don't be worried in the event that you hear that your Japanese Bobtail cat has this condition in the event that it ever comes about.

f. Hypertrophic cardiomyopathy
Hypertrophic cardiomyopathy, or HCM, can cause the heart muscle to become too thick. This is a difficult concern and it is often hard to prevent. In fact, there is no way how a breeder can have a HCM-free line. An echocradiogram can develop if a cat has this condition but it is one that will still be random. Any cat with HCM should not be added into any breeding line in order to at least reduce the potential for this condition to move from one cat to the next.

g. Liver amyloidosis
Many Japanese Bobtail lines, particularly those that are mixed with some breeds based from well outside the United States like the Oriental Shorthair, have been known to struggle with liver amyloidosis. This is a condition where a protein can build up within the liver. This can often cause organ failure. Any cat that is known to suffer from liver amyolidosis must be removed from any breeding line. This is due to how the condition is extremely difficult to manage or treat.

There are also other age related disorders that you should be aware of, just like human beings, as the cats grow older, so does their immunity. At this stage they are more vulnerable and prone to opportunistic diseases. Considering age as an immediate factor will also allow you to understand the frequent medical disorders that your cat faces. So in as much as you want to consider your cat stronger, be cautious and think twice upon its age.

6) Spaying and Neutering

Controlled animal breeding is very essential. Different people have different tastes for different animal sexes. While some would prefer male pets, others would love to be associated with the female. All these may just emanate from the fact that both male and female breeds of animals are portrayed to possess different characteristics.

The male can be rough and physical while the female might become overly sexual. Spaying and neutering is needed to ensure that such traits are to be kept in check and to be less likely to remain evident over time.

Spaying and neutering are special procedures carried out by prominent veterinarians to ensure that the cat is incapable of reproducing by removing the necessary organs. In the female cats, the fallopian tube, the uterus and the ovaries are removed while in the male, castration and removal of testicles is practiced. In

Chapter 13: Caring for the Japanese Bobtail

females this process is known as spaying while in the males it is known as neutering.

We have had quite a rising number of abandoned cats being taken in by animal control systems. You may also want to maintain only a specific number of cats as pets. Irrespective of the number you choose, you will not desire whatsoever to find your cat roaming further from home or you may not desire to find a spontaneous rise in their numbers overnight.

A healthy, well-taken care of pet is an image you may wish to gallantly sell across the streets. Who doesn't love to be associated with success in any field anyway? This is the more reason why spaying and neutering simply comes in handy in control of the cat's breeding.

Feline overpopulation is a common problem these days. Even with a predominantly indoor cat like the Japanese Bobtail, there are chances that the cat will mate with other strays. This may lead to kittens either in your home or in the streets. This is a problem either way as feline overpopulation has very painful and sad consequences.

It is true that several shelters are euthanizing cats to make room for homeless kittens and also kittens that have been rescued.

If every cat owner takes the responsibility of neutering and spaying seriously, these unpleasant conditions can be controlled to a large extent.

a. How to Spay or Neuter
Like any other domesticated animal of its kind, a spaying operation involves the veterinarian providing general anesthetics with the surgical removal of the ovaries from the uterus through an incision made at the belly of the cat. Usually, the vet will ask you to withhold food for at least 12 hours prior to the surgery in order to minimize potential anesthetic complications.

Chapter 13: Caring for the Japanese Bobtail

For the castration of the male, the incisions are made on the scrotum to remove the ovaries, and the food doesn't necessarily have to be withheld. The cats will usually recover from this neutering process very quickly, come the following day after surgery, they should be up and well again, but if yours is unusually quiet, please show concern and inform your vet immediately.

b. When to Spay or Neuter
If you intend to get someone to spay or neuter your cat, you should do it before it gets a litter or even its first heat. The process of spaying or neutering is best done before the cat reaches puberty. You should also note that your cat can be spayed as a kitten but not before it reaches at least 8 weeks or if it weighs less than two pounds. In fact in America, the American Veterinary Medical Association supports early spaying and neutering as the best period possible for any of the two to be carried out. Completely armed with this knowledge, you will appreciate the subsequent reasons for spaying and neutering.

In case you have neglected this important consideration, you can even take your cat to the vet when he or she is in heat. However, with female cats, spaying when they are in heat will lead to excessive blood loss. If you think that you want your adult cat to be neutered or spayed, you can consult your vet about the safety of the procedure.

c. Improved Quality
If you are a person who only wants to have a cat as a pet, you may just find this reason really fulfilling. See, humanity has been modifying domesticated animals to better suit their human needs for centuries. With controlled propagation of selected animal breeds to improve quality, man has achieved greater milestones in successful animal breeding. Just like culling that deals with sorting out animals bred by removing the smaller and weaker animals and concentrates on breeding the much better quality, spaying and neutering does the same only in a different way, through making your cat barren or impotent.

Chapter 13: Caring for the Japanese Bobtail

This in turn will help your cat to harness energy. You see, cats are very agile and playful pets. As a completely active cat, the male may become wild by wandering away from home in pursuit of the female, to quench its desire to mate. The female on the other hand will be having kittens after every successful gestation. In both cases, the cats use a lot of energy and this makes their health rapidly deteriorate, leaving you with an emaciated cat for a pet.

However, when the cat is neutered, the cat's needs are limited and it grows stronger, bigger and healthier. In fact, even its life span is improved, movement controlled and therefore it's not vulnerable to diseases.

No matter what surgical procedure your cat is going to undergo, a good amount of preparation is mandatory. You can get all the necessary pre-surgical advice from your vet. Make sure you adhere to all the guidelines. The most common precaution to take is to ensure that your cat does not eat anything after midnight until the surgery.

If you are taking a kitten for operation, on the other hand, the nutritional requirements are drastically different. Following these measures will ensure that there are no complications during the surgery and after.

d. Controlled Breeding

Cats can also be kept for breeding purposes. If you are choosing a cat for this very reason, you may want to go for the best. Yet again it's not every single day that you will want your cat to breed, if you are not doing so for commercial purposes, or even if you were, there will reach a point that you will consider the number of cats in your yard to be enough. Or so it will come to pass that you will want to control a lesser breed and maintain the better one or that you will consider your cat's age to be less ideal if conceived.

These reasons will allow you to look for a controlled system of breeding, and spaying just provides the remedy. Either way, as a

Chapter 13: Caring for the Japanese Bobtail

cat owner you will only get to achieve either your ideal number of cats, or your ideal type of breed, meticulous, right?

e. Reduced Hostility
No one likes a hostile pet. Everyone likes his or her pet-cat to be subtle, warm, welcoming, and very easy to relate to. While this is the case it is not the reality, you will find most cats that have not been spayed quite hostile and very much hot blooded. This reason is attributed to their desire for the opposite sex.

Neutering will therefore be a very viable way to reduce your cat's hostility. This prevents your cat from exposing itself to dangerous situations such as catfights over a mating partner. Your cat will therefore become friendlier to you and to your loved ones. In fact by the end of this process, you can enjoy the comfort of your home, knowing that even your children are safe from the constant cat claws.

There is no apparent change in the cat's personality after neutering or spaying. It is true that the cat might be quiet and calm and not too playful for a while but he or she will get back to its original self as soon as it recovers.

There are several myths that currently suggest that a Japanese Bobtail cat will become lethargic or obese after neutering or spaying. This prevents most people from considering this rather important procedure.

You may have to provide your cat with a certain diet after neutering or spaying. This is to ensure that the cat gets all the nutrients and calories required during the recovery process. If you have any concerns about the process of neutering or spaying, your vet will be able to provide you with all possible details.

f. Reduced Infections
Usually cats experience even their first heat much earlier than anticipated. If you take the advantage and neuter your cat early, it will save it from cancerous diseases, that can either be transmitted by other cats to it or other infections that may be acquired due to

Chapter 13: Caring for the Japanese Bobtail

lack of hygiene. This is a good advantage that will be to the benefit of every cat including the Japanese Bobtail.

7) Vaccinations

There are core vaccines that every cat must have and then there are some that are for specific breeds, called non-core vaccines.

You need to ensure that your veterinarian can provide your cat with these vaccinations. Only a veterinarian can administer them.

Panleukopenia should be given strictly between 6 to 8 weeks. This one will be given to your cat before you take it in. It puts off the fear of the cat being exposed to it at home that may make it fall sick or infect it in any possible way before it adapts to its new environment.

After being administered that very first time, the vaccine is to be administered again after every 3 to 4 weeks until the kitten gets to week 16. This very first vaccine is always combined with feline viral respiratory disease complex vaccines in one dose.

1 or 2 years later, cats who love to mix with other cats are given a booster that will boost their immunity. The Japanese Bobtail should also be taken care of in this manner. In fact, it is suggested that it should have all the three sets of vaccines since it is the most outgoing and affectionate of all cat breeds.

The rabies vaccine must also be used at 8 to 12 weeks. It may also be required every couple of years to ensure that the cat will stay protected from this threatening condition.

Vaccinations are important for all animals, especially home pets, and have immense benefits that will help you recognize what a beautiful cat you have for a pet. Even though it is specifically intended for the cat, you will find that such vaccinations can have greater underlying benefits for you too if not also for your household. Therefore much attention should be paid while to the

Chapter 13: Caring for the Japanese Bobtail

timetable for when your veterinarian is going to provide your cat with the vaccinations.

Be sure to talk with your veterinarian about the vaccinations your cat will need. If you are uncertain as to when your cat's vaccination schedule has been followed then you might need to take a look at getting boosters. In addition, you need to talk with a breeder about any vaccinations that your cat might have received in order to ensure that you've got a cat that is fully up to schedule in terms of the necessary vaccinations that one needs.

a. Fighting Infections
As a cat lover, you must have guessed that such benefits would come with vaccination. Vaccines help your cat in boosting its immune system, helping your cat to fight infections; it ensures that the disease-causing microorganisms become obsolete. Within most of these vaccines are dead microorganisms that when administered into your cat's immune system produce proteins called antibodies, so that when your cat encounters the actual living microorganisms those antibodies "fight" the infection.

These antibodies will therefore have your cat's back. Kittens are even more vulnerable to these diseases since their immune systems are not totally developed and their only remedy is the vaccination. Though they still get some antibodies from their already vaccinated mothers through the breast milk, vaccination proves that it still wheels around the chain of the cat's lives and health.

b. Preservation of Breeds
The Japanese Bobtail has to be preserved quite well so its unique traits are going to remain prevalent. The right sense of precaution is needed to ensure that there will be no problems coming out of whatever it is you are trying to manage. Vaccinations are done as a means of helping to ensure that the breed will continue to exist for years to come.

8) After Vaccination, What's Next?

Typically, cats, just like humans, may experience side effects when antibodies are introduced to their system. These side effects usually vary and should be no cause for alarm as they always knock them off. However, if they become persistent, a vet's advice must be rapidly sought.

The side effects can develop within hours of vaccination. Milder side effects may include swelling and discomfort at the vaccination site, lethargy, or decreased appetite. However, the more serious symptoms that occur less often would be persistent vomiting, diarrhea, severe breathing difficulties, or eventual collapse.

These require you to always put your doctor on alert, as they can be life threatening or suddenly just turn to instant emergencies. With the swelling of vaccination areas, this may last for up to weeks later. If it doesn't disappear in two weeks, seek medical attention.

In rare cases, your cat might need an operation. Your cat might experience a little discomfort after these processes. These procedures very seldom have a painful recovery process. If it is in pain, you must make sure you either leave it under specialized care or consult your vet regularly. There are a few precautions that you can take to ensure that the recovery process is comfortable and safe.

Give your cat a safe place in the house to rest during the recovery process. This place should not be accessible by other pets or even children.

Do not encourage jumping or running during this recovery process. You can take it out on walks but make sure that he/she is not physically exerted.

The area that has been operated upon should not be licked. So, getting your cat an Elizabethan collar is the best option.

Chapter 13: Caring for the Japanese Bobtail

During the recovery process, avoid using litter in the litter box. Instead, use shredded paper. The problem with sand or litter is that the dust can cause unwanted infections.

The site with the incision must be cleaned regularly to avoid infections.

You must always look out for symptoms like:

Redness in the site of incision

Swelling in the site of incision

Discharge from the area

Reduced appetite

Vomiting

Lethargy

If you do notice one or more symptoms, inform your vet to improve the recovery process.

Chapter 14: Finding a Good Vet

You will find a lot of online videos about the Japanese Bobtail cat these days. In any case, it is necessary for you to have a reliable vet who you can trust with your pet. It is never a good idea to constantly change the vet who treats your Japanese Bobtail cat. After all, these cats do not necessarily appreciate change. They are usually reluctant to cooperate with vets. This is regardless of the breed you've got to bear with; the Japanese Bobtail is clearly a good example of this.

You must give your cat time to get accustomed to the touch and voice of one vet. Once he/she is comfortable with him or her, your cat will be more relaxed during vet visits. A vet is an important part of your cat's life and you must make sure you look for the perfect one to take care of your pet.

There will be several large and small veterinary clinics around your town. So, it can be quite confusing when you set out to choose something for your precious pet.

The best way to look for a vet is to ask for recommendations from your friends and neighbors. If you know people in the neighborhood who have had pets for a long time, they will be able to recommend someone to you.

You must make a conscious effort to look for someone who is specialized in cat care. The section of veterinary care is growing rapidly and you will definitely find someone in the vicinity.

In order to be prepared for an emergency, here are some things that you might want to consider before you zero in on one vet:

How far is your vet from your home?

Is the commuting time too long?

In case of an emergency, will you make it on time to the vet?

Chapter 14: Finding a Good Vet

Is the ambiance of the clinic feasible for your cat?

It is always better to find someone close to your house. It must not take more than 15 minutes to drive down to your vet. Even if it is not an emergency, remember that your cat is not particularly fond of long drives.

Once you have found someone who seems to fit into all the requirements, you can make a trial visit. The chemistry between your cat and the vet is extremely important if you want to make it a long lasting relationship.

There are some signs that will indicate how comfortable you and your pet will be in a particular clinic. Make the following observations if you are visiting for the first time:

The waiting room must be well maintained.

The ambiance must be comforting for the cat so that it feels secure when being examined.

If it is a common clinic for dogs and cats, how are they maintained when they are admitted for hospital care? Are they kept in separate cages?

The people at the reception must be friendly. These people are going to be your point of contact in the coming sessions and you must be comfortable with them.

Once you are in the examination room, check how the vet interacts with pets and their owners. The tone must be soothing. It must be able to provide undivided attention to your cat. The vet must value your opinions about your cat's health and must be respectful towards you.

The personality of your vet plays an important role in the way it interacts with the animals. The vet must be genuinely passionate about the job. Without passion, you cannot be assured that he/she will go to all lengths to ensure the best for your cat. He/she must be good with cats. He/she must have complete knowledge on the different practices and techniques that have evolved in veterinary practices. He/she must also make a conscious effort to upgrade his skills and knowledge.

Once you are assured of the behavior of the vet towards you and your cat, you need to get down to the technical and legal aspects.

Is the facility adept in handling emergencies?

How many cages or rooms do they have for the pets that have been admitted there?

Is every staff member educated?

Is the facility licensed?

What are the costs for tests and surgeries?

Is the pricing competitive enough?

What are the insurance policies that they accept?

How many emergencies are handled after regular working hours?

Who takes care of the pets when they are hospitalized?

Are they open to alternative medicines and treatments?

Once you have received satisfactory answers to all the above questions, you can be assured that this facility is best suited for your cat. Remember, the person whom you choose as your vet is going to be your partner in the well being of your beautiful cat.

Preparing your Cat for a Vet Visit

Taking a cat to the vet is not easy. If you ask other pet owners, they will tell you that it is definitely not the picnic that you expect it to be. Unknown to most people, cats experience a lot of stress when they are travelling. As a result, it is best that you prepare your cat well for a visit to the vet. Here are five tips that will make the visit less stressful for your cat:

Chapter 14: Finding a Good Vet

Create a pre-vet routine. Even cats require a good amount of mental preparation before they are taken to the vet. Start by giving your cat a thorough check up from head to toe. This can only be an imitation of the actual test that will take place in the vet's clinic. The idea is to get the cat used to being handled by the vet.

Getting your cat used to the carrier is another way to making the visit less stressful. If your cat learns to associate the carrier with vet visits, it might resist the visit. On the other hand, if you create associations like playtime or even outdoor visits with the carrier, your cat might look forward to the positive activities and be less stressed. You can designate the carrier as a nap place. Throw in its favourite toys and treats inside the carrier to attract your cat towards it.

Of course, the actual journey to the vet is going to create a great deal of stress in the cat. You can reduce this by being affectionate during the drive. Play with it and pet it on the way to keep anxiety levels down.

Make your car cat friendly. Most of the resistance to the visit to the vet is not the clinic itself. It has more to do with the journey to the vet. Usually, cats are taken out in the car only during their visit to the vet. As a result, they automatically associate cars with the negative experiences that they might have had at the vet, including injections and bad tasting medicines. So cats can never stay calm and relaxed inside a car.

However, you can help your cat make positive associations by including drives in the car in your daily routine. You can take the cat for short distances too. Take the car to the park, for instance. Then your cat will stop making negative associations. You can even stop by at the vet's clinic for 5 minutes to get your cat used to the staff there.

Chapter 14: Finding a Good Vet

The basic idea is to get your cat used to the car. It must learn to be calm and relaxed during these visits. Keeping some toys in the car and allowing it to play during these drives will also help a great deal.

Beat the waiting room blues. One place dreaded by all animals is the waiting room at the clinic. There are several unpleasant sounds like the barking of dogs and even chatter of humans that increase the levels of anxiety in a cat.

Cats are, by nature, solitary animals and do not like being introduced to so many strange sights and sounds at one go. The best thing to do would be to leave your cat in the carrier until it is called in for examination. This gives it a secure hide out and it will be more at ease.

Make sure that the carrier that you are using is large enough. Place a nice cat bed or a cushion inside for it to rest on. You can also leave toys and goodies inside the carrier. A top-loading carrier is a must, as it will become impossible for you to get your frightened kitty out of a front-loading one.

Special pheromone sprays are available to reduce anxiety and stress in cats during their visit to the vet. These sprays imitate the scent that cats leave when they rub themselves against the legs of their loved ones.

You can also schedule your appointments to the less busy parts of the day. That way, the chaos in the waiting room will be lesser, making your cat feel more relaxed.

Get friendly with your vet. It is good to allow your vet to spend some time with your cat and break the ice. Of course, the vet is going to poke and prod the cat for examination. This becomes less stressful if the cat can look at the vet as a friend rather than a stranger.

Chapter 14: Finding a Good Vet

Make sure you clear up all queries related to your cat's well being when you visit the vet. Even if it means additional visits, do not shy away from it.

Send items from home for overnight stays. If your cat is due for overnight hospital care, send its favourite items from home. The idea is to keep him/her around familiar scents so that he/she does not get too anxious. There are several routine procedures like neutering that can be extremely stressful for your cat. Making regular visits and sending him/her things from home can really help the cat overcome this anxiety.

You must always work with your vet to ensure the complete well being of your cat. You must trust the knowledge and expertise of your vet if you want him/her to be the best caregiver for your cat.

Usually, vets will be more than willing to lend support in the form of study material to help you understand how you can take care of your cat at home.

Chapter 15: The Cost of Owning a Japanese Bobtail

Now that you are aware of the basics of cat care, you might begin to wonder how expensive it is to actually take care of one. In comparison to dogs, cats are cheaper to own. However, if you want to put a number on your cat care expenses, here is a clear break up.

1) Initial Costs

Your Cat
$600 (£380) at the least.
Due to its overall rarity outside of Japan, a Japanese Bobtail can cost about $600 or £380 on average. In some cases you might spend less money for the cat if it does not have much of a noticeable look to its tail. Still, you might spend less money if you adopt a cat; some adoption fees may be charged but they are often less than what you might expect from a breeder.

Vaccinations and de-sexing may be covered in some cases but this is not always going to be the concern. Always look to see what a breeder or other place does with regards to getting help from a veterinarian in the process of vaccinating and de-sexing the cat.

Council Registration
$40 (£5)
Every cat needs to be registered under the local council in certain countries. This is necessary to obtain required licenses for your cat.

Desexing
$100-200 (£60 - 120)
This is only if your breeder hasn't taken care of this already. The costs vary from one vet to another. Spaying or neutering is always going to be important to consider.

Chapter 15: The Cost of Owning a Japanese Bobtail

Microchipping
$50 (£30)
In some countries, microchipping is mandatory. This is a good option to ensure that your cat, if lost, can be reunited with you at the earliest. This works in that a microchip material will be implanted into a safe part of the cat's body. It will be found under the cat's skin.

The authorities can use a device to read the data for which the cat is listed to ensure that it will be found and returned to its proper owner over time.

Vaccinations
$50-$70 (£30 - 50)
Never ignore or neglect vaccinations. Refer to the section on vaccinations for more information.

Cat Carriers
$30-$50 (£20 - 30)
You will definitely need a cat carrier to make trips to the vet or travel with your beloved cat.

2) Optional Expenses

Scratching Post
$100 approx (£60)
If you want to safeguard your home from havoc, make sure you get your kitty a scratch post. The costs may be higher depending upon the type of post you choose.

Cat Toys
$30 for basics (£20)
There are so many toys available on the market that you can certainly not put a price on this. However, for a basic selection, you will pay about $30 or £20. You must not neglect cat toys, as they are necessary for good exercise for your cat.

Chapter 15: The Cost of Owning a Japanese Bobtail

3) Ongoing Costs

Food
$10 per week (£6)
There are various brands that you get on the market. The price of the cat food will depend entirely upon what you choose to feed your cat.

Litter
$8 per week (£5)
This is just an approximation. The costs may vary as per the type of litter.

Worming Medications
$2.50 per week (£1.50)
These topical medicines need to be re-applied regularly.

Veterinary checks
$70 per year (£60)
This is the cost for routine checkups only. It does not account for unexpected accidents of illnesses.

Pet Sitter
$10 - 25 per day (£6 - 15)
This is an expense that you cannot rule out if you are someone who travels occasionally or even works late.

Owning a pet is a big responsibility monetarily. It is as good as having a baby at home. If you think that you might have to compromise on any of the expenses mentioned above, make sure you re-think your decision of bringing home a cat like this.

4) Insurance

You might also consider taking insurance for your cat. It can cover many expenses that are associated with taking care of your cat and making sure that it stays as healthy as possible. Usually,

Chapter 15: The Cost of Owning a Japanese Bobtail

insurance policies are anything between $20 / £12 and $60 / £36 per month. Please be aware that the monthly cost for insurance might increase each year, as your cat gets older.

Chapter 16: Care for an Aging Cat

Major milestones have been achieved in the last decade or so when it comes to treatment of cat diseases and management of cat health conditions. Improvements of existing cat medications and discovery of new cat treatment methods has made it possible for cats to live much longer than their expected lifespan.

Although all cats of all ages benefit from such improvements, aging cats happen to be the biggest beneficiaries. This is because properly cared for aging cats can now age gracefully without necessarily experiencing the pain and a lot of discomfort that aging cats hitherto experienced in the past.

Although your cat generally has a lifespan of up to 15 years in a majority of cases, it can live to attain the age of 20 years and slightly above so long as you provide it with proper care including veterinary care.

1) What is aging?

Aging is a process that every living being goes through. It is a natural process that sets in when life expectancy is attained. One day in a cat's life is a very long time taking into account the fact that a year in a cat's life is similar to about 15 years for humans. Likewise, a cat aged 15 years is like a human being aged 85 years. Just like in humans, the onset of aging in cats brings with it several challenges, some which can make your cat very uncomfortable if you do not offer the necessary help.

2) Physiological and Behavioural Changes

Your Japanese Bobtail cat will exhibit many changes once it attains old age. One of the most visible changes is the tendency to

Chapter 16: Caring for an Aging Cat

walk on its hocks. This is because its hind leg muscles become weak to a point where running and jumping becomes difficult. This is the time to change its bed to a larger one because it finds it difficult to curl up in a small bed. Your aging cat will also be very forgetful. It may choose to remain outdoors in case it ventures out regardless of the weather. This is also the time when it can easily get lost in case it is used to venturing out without company.

A visible sign of aging in cats is usually what is referred to as winding down. This is when it grows thinner with its hip, shoulder and backbones becoming visible. In addition to becoming thinner, the fat layer just under the skin also melts away, further exposing the bones. It is important at this stage to consult a vet for advice on special types of cat food and dietary supplements to feed your cat on.

The aging process also causes many faculty changes in a cat's life. Its hearing and cognition abilities diminish to a great extent. Furthermore, its metabolic rate also decreases. In case your Japanese Bobtail is not used to venturing outdoors, it is bound to feel cold most of the time. It is your responsibility to ensure that your cat sleeps in warm bed materials. Make sure it gets plenty of exposure to the sun's rays too.

One fact you need to remain alert to when your cat ages is the fact that its immunity reduces, making it highly susceptible to many infections. It becomes very necessary to take your cat to a vet whenever you notice any strange behaviour or symptoms for immediate vet care.

Although Japanese Bobtail cats are people-oriented pets, your aging Bobtail will seek attention more often as it gets older. This is because it naturally knows that it is incapacitated in many ways and will want to be near you most of the time for comfort, assurance and help. Your cat will however tend to sleep for a much longer time.

Chapter 16: Caring for an Aging Cat

Because of the many behavioural and physiological changes that your cat is bound to go through once the aging process sets in, it is most likely to engage less in physical activities. It is however very important that you exercise your cat's mind. Limited physical exercise is also necessary to help your cat overcome any discomfort it may experience because of such diseases as arthritis, which aging cats are highly susceptible to.

3) Health Challenges in Old Cats

Your aging Japanese Bobtail cat will experience a lot of changes including reduced immunity. This exposes it to many diseases/health conditions that you must take note of with the aim of helping it cope. Some of the health challenges your cat is most likely to face include:

Parasite Infestation
Your aging Japanese Bobtail cat will probably not groom itself as it used to do. This exposes it to parasite infestation and in particular ticks and fleas. This will likely happen if it is used to going outdoors. Infestation of these parasites will easily lead to skin infections. The likelihood of your cat becoming anaemic also becomes high. This is when it becomes necessary to use flea spray or powder. Although you have the alternative of using flea collars, they have the disadvantage of being ineffective. Furthermore, flea collars can also cause allergic reaction.

Your cat is also likely to have internal parasites in case it is used to going outdoors, just in the same way it used to do when it was a kitten. It becomes necessary for your aging cat to receive treatment for worms and in particular roundworms after every three months.

Blindness
In addition to such health challenges as hearing loss and loss of memory, a major challenge that your aging Japanese Bobtail is likely to face is blindness. This starts as partial loss of vision before developing into total blindness.

Chapter 16: Caring for an Aging Cat

Although you may not be able to know when your cat is losing its vision, there are specific signs you need to look out for. These include reluctance to move, misjudging heights, clumsiness, eye rubbing, large pupils and when it easily gets startled. Because treating blindness due to old age is simply impossible, the best you can do to help your cat cope is ensure that it moves in a secure environment, offer help all the time and speaking to it often.

Pain
Such diseases/health conditions as arthritis that your aging Japanese Bobtail is susceptible to are usually accompanied with pain. Your cat may tremble, shiver or crouch. It becomes very important to understand your cat's body language with the aim of offering help. It becomes necessary to take your cat to a vet for proper diagnosis of existing disease and for appropriate pain medications.

Dental Infections
Old cats are highly susceptible to dental infections. About 70% of all old cats suffer from dental infections mostly caused by the formation of plaque. It is during your cat's old age that you must ensure that it receives regular dental care that involves removal of plaque that forms tartar, which in effect leads to gingivitis.

Arthritis
Arthritis is the most common health problem that cats in old age suffer from, just like in humans. This health condition is usually accompanied by joint pain, pain that can make your cat very uncomfortable. Your cat will find it very difficult to engage in physical activities. The best way to help your cat cope is to consult with a local vet for the best supplements to buy; supplements that support the rebuilding of joint cartilage.

Reduced Heart Function
Just like in humans, your cat's heart function reduces once old age sets in. Its heart muscles do not only weaken but also enlarge. It

becomes necessary to take your cat to a vet for regular checkups and medications that strengthen heart muscles.

4) What to Do With an Old Japanese Bobtail Cat

Living with an old cat can be a serious challenge, especially if it becomes senile. You simply will not cope with the amount of care it needs to continue living comfortably. It is because of this that you may look for alternative ways on how your cat can still receive proper care until when it dies. You have three options:

Cat Rescue Centre
Taking your aged Japanese Bobtail cat to a dedicated cat rescue centre may be your only option of letting your aged cat go. Although it can be very difficult, doing so will lessen your burden of having to watch over it all the time.

Cat rescue centres are institutions established by such organizations as animal welfare societies. Such centres are usually staffed with qualified pet personnel with the necessary skills on taking care of pets of all ages. In addition to admitting aged pets including cats at a small fee, they also offer younger pets for adoption. Such do include rescued pets or those born in such institutions.

Most cat rescue centres are funded by donations received from pet lovers and other organizations. Some well established cat rescue centres serve as educational institutions where pet lovers have the opportunity to learn more about pets they are interested in buying or adopting. Taking your old Japanese Bobtail to a cat rescue centre does not in any way mean disposing it off. Most rescue centres allow owners to visit their aged cats. This makes for a good opportunity to reconnect with pets they have lived with for a long time.

Chapter 16: Caring for an Aging Cat

Euthanasia

Euthanasia is the other route or option you have when it comes to dealing with your old cat. Most cat owners whose cats are aged choose to have their cats euthanized instead of taking them to cat rescue centres. The main reason for this is the fact that having their cats euthanized eliminates the worry they would otherwise continuously have over their pets at such centres.

Simply put, euthanasia is the practice where life is ended. You may choose to have your aged cat euthanized in order to relieve it from the pain, anguish, suffering and discomfort it goes through as it waits for its natural death. Different jurisdictions have different laws relating to euthanasia for humans and pets. Your vet should be in a good position to enlighten you on what laws apply in your jurisdiction.

Just like in the case of humans, a vet will normally require that you sign a consent form before euthanizing your cat. The signing of the form absolves a vet from any claim you make thereafter that he/she caused your cat's death. There are however certain instances where vets request pet owners for permission to euthanize their aged pets. Such cases are usually when vets discover serious diseases in the cause of treating cats. Even in such situations, cat owners have the last word on whether or not their cats should be euthanized.

Whether you take your cat to a vet clinic to be euthanized or call a vet to undertake the procedure at home, the procedure is the same. The procedure normally involves giving an over-dose of anaesthesia into the main vein in one of its forelegs. In case of difficult or troublesome cats, a crush cage is normally used. Injection of anaesthesia leads to immediate unconsciousness followed by slow death. Your cat is most likely to exhale and pass urine as body muscles relax after death. To ensure that your cat is indeed dead, a vet may give additional injection of anaesthesia into the kidney or the heart. Your lovely cat will most likely die with eyes open and a vet will simply close the eyes before placing

Chapter 16: Caring for an Aging Cat

the cat in a position where it appears to be just asleep. It is only after this that a vet wraps your cat in a black bag both for safety and privacy before handing it over to you.

Watching your cat die can be a very traumatizing experience. The experience can remain in your mind for a very long time. This is why some cat owners choose to remain in a separate room when a vet undertakes euthanasia on their aged cats and other pets.
Most cat owners do choose to call a vet to perform the procedure in their homes rather than at a vet's clinic, a move that you too may consider. This is because having the procedure undertaken at home is somehow less traumatic. The cost of euthanasia varies from one region to another and from one vet to another. The cost can actually be on the higher side if you choose to call a vet to undertake the procedure at home. Generally, the cost ranges between $30 and $80 (£17- £35) across the world. It is always recommended that you settle any outstanding amount with a vet before he/she undertakes the procedure. This is because you may not find it comfortable talking about payments when your cat is already dead.

Home Care
You may choose not to take your aged Japanese Bobtail to a cat rescue centre or have it euthanized. You may take this route if you are fond of your cat and have the time to provide it with all the necessary care it needs until it dies natural death. Although most cat owners choose to care for their cats at home until they die, the suffering, pain and anguish they go through can similarly be traumatizing. Taking your aged cat to a cat rescue centre may eliminate your responsibility to dispose of the body when it finally dies. This will depend on the agreement between you and a care centre management. Most centres do undertake to dispose of bodies of dead cats. Depending on your arrangement, you may be informed. Having your cat euthanized at a vet's clinic, at home or if you choose to care for your cat at home, you will have to determine how to dispose of the body.

Chapter 16: Caring for an Aging Cat

Body Disposal
There are a number of ways through which you can dispose of your Japanese Bobtail cat's body. Below are just some of the ways:

Burial
Burial of pets is fast becoming popular around the world and it is highly possible that you too may choose to bury your Japanese Bobtail cat when it finally dies. Even so, you need to acquaint yourself with your local by-laws that relate to disposal of dead pet bodies. You will need to bury your cat soon enough before it putrefies unless you have a freezer where you can store the body for a few days. You may choose to bury your cat in your back garden or at your local authority's pet cemetery.
Even so, there are instances when you may not be allowed to bury your cat. Such are instances where the body poses a degree of risk to human health. This may apply if your cat dies of rabies in which case it will be the responsibility of a vet to dispose of the body.

Cremation
Like with burial, cremation is another popular way of disposing of dead bodies. You may choose to have your cat's body cremated to give you the opportunity to bring its ashes home in a jar to scatter in its room/space or simply keep. It is common to find pet cemeteries having pet cremation facilities where you can have your cat cremated.

Taxidermy
You may choose to have your cat handled through a taxidermist to at least allow you have it at home although in a static state. Taxidermy is a process where a professional taxidermist removes all the cat's internal organs including tissue and bones. The remaining skin is then stuffed to make your dead cat look real.

Chapter 16: Caring for an Aging Cat

Desiccation
At times referred to as freeze-drying, desiccation is the process where water is removed from your cat's body. Your cat will simply be put in the right posture before being desiccated. The process can take as long as six months and most cat owners do like the result because of its lifelike nature. Because of environmental factors, the desiccated body is usually housed in a glass container for preservation. This gives you the opportunity to have your cat at home even though it is actually dead.

Resin Preservation
This is another way you may choose to dispose of your dead Japanese Bobtail cat's body. It involves the removal of blood and other body fluids, which are then replaced with resin. Resin has the characteristic of setting in to a solid, which in effect yields a lifelike body.

Post-Disposal Period
The period soon after disposing of your cat's body can be a very trying time. It can indeed be a trying time in case you have another Japanese Bobtail cat and other pets at home. Do cats have feelings? Will they realize that one of them is missing? How will they cope knowing that one of them is missing? It is a fact that cats have feelings. Japanese Bobtail cats in particular develop a strong bond between them and will therefore be troubled with the absence of one of their own.

One thing you may notice when you have two Japanese Bobtail cats as pets is that each of them can mark their own territory. One of them naturally becomes the leader of the other. The absence of one of them therefore traumatizes the remaining one. It may take some time before the remaining one adjusts. The best way to comfort the remaining one is to always give it as much attention as possible.

The situation can be very complicated to handle in case you have children. This is because Japanese Bobtail cats get along very

Chapter 16: Caring for an Aging Cat

well with children because of their playful nature. Your dead cat will not have just been your kids' companion but a valuable playmate. They are bound to take its death very hard. The best you can do in such a situation is to make your kids understand what death is and why their playmate has died.

Making your kids understand what death is and that it applies to human beings can be very beneficial to them. This is because kids learn through experiences and knowing about death will make them appreciate the fact that death is natural and can happen to any family member at any time.

5) How to Cope with Your Japanese Bobtail Cat's Death

Your cat's death can be similar to the death of your child or a young family member. Knowing that you adopted or bought it, nurtured it to maturity and that it was a valuable companion that is no more can take a toll on your mind. Not only will you develop a feeling of loss but will grieve for your cat. You will probably go into a state of denial, develop anger and mourn before accepting that your lovely Japanese Bobtail cat is no more. This may be the appropriate time to share your feelings with other family members. Doing so will no doubt go a long way in overcoming your anger and feelings of loss you may develop.

One reason why many cat owners choose to dispose of the bodies of their cats is to have the opportunity to remember their cats knowing that it is buried in their backyards. Remembrance provides you and your family with a good opportunity to reflect back on the good times you had with your dead cat.

6) Replacing Your Dead Japanese Bobtail Cat

Having lived with an Japanese Bobtail cat that is no more will most likely drive you to adopt or buy another to replace the dead one. When to have another one will however depend on several

Chapter 16: Caring for an Aging Cat

factors. One of the most important factors that may make it necessary to have another Japanese Bobtail soon after the death of the previous one is if you had two of them.

The loneliness that the remaining one will feel may make it necessary to get another one for company. You may also need to have another one soon after in case you have children. The other reason why you may need to replace your dead cat soon relates to why you bought or adopted the dead one in the first place. You may simply like pets and Japanese Bobtails in particular. You may also be used to having a pet as a companion and cannot do without one.

Conclusion

The Japanese Bobtail is different from many other cats thanks to its unique tail design. This makes it rather different from others but it also goes to show that it is a cat breed that is very unique and special when compared with others.

The extreme intelligence that the cat exhibits is also amazing to spot. The cat will certainly make friends with you, other people in the house and even other cats. In addition, it can be found in many colours and markings.

Naturally, it will be a real challenge for you to find any breeder that works with this cat in mind, what with the fact that the breed's history outside of Japan is not all that vast. Still, you need to make sure that you are careful when looking for a breeder or at least looking in any spot for such a cat as this. This is to ensure that the cat will be healthy and that you've got one that you know will be safe to have.

This cat is intelligent and fun to be around but you must always be certain that you are careful around it. Make sure the cat is treated right and that you take care of its coat and diet with plenty of attention in mind. Make sure you also watch for how your cat behaves and that you understand what you need to do as the cat ages.

If you understand what you need to do with your cat then you will see over time that your Japanese Bobtail will be a friend for life. This is a truly fascinating cat breed worth exploring.

Published by IMB Publishing 2015

Copyright and Trademarks: This publication is Copyrighted 2015 by IMB Publishing. All products, publications, software and services mentioned and recommended in this publication are protected by trademarks. In such instance, all trademarks & copyright belong to the respective owners. All rights reserved. No part of this book may be reproduced or transferred in any form or by any means, graphic, electronic, or mechanical, including photocopying, recording, taping, or by any information storage retrieval system, without the written permission of the authors. Pictures used in this book are either royalty free pictures bought from stock-photo websites or have the source mentioned underneath the picture.

Disclaimer and Legal Notice: This product is not legal or medical advice and should not be interpreted in that manner. You need to do your own due-diligence to determine if the content of this product is right for you. The author and the affiliates of this product are not liable for any damages or losses associated with the content in this product. While every attempt has been made to verify the information shared in this publication, neither the author nor the affiliates assume any responsibility for errors, omissions or contrary interpretation of the subject matter herein. Any perceived slights to any specific person(s) or organization(s) are purely unintentional. We have no control over the nature, content and availability of the web sites listed in this book. The inclusion of any web site links does not necessarily imply a recommendation or endorse the views expressed within them. IMB Publishing takes no responsibility for, and will not be liable for, the websites being temporarily unavailable or being removed from the Internet. The accuracy and completeness of information provided herein and opinions stated herein are not guaranteed or warranted to produce any particular results, and the advice and strategies, contained herein may not be suitable for every individual. The author shall not be liable for any loss incurred as a consequence of the use and application, directly or indirectly, of any information presented in this work. This publication is designed to provide information in regards to the subject matter covered. The information included in this book has been compiled to give an overview of the subject s and detail some of the symptoms, treatments etc. that are available to people with this condition. It is not intended to give medical advice. For a firm diagnosis of your condition, and for a treatment plan suitable for you, you should consult your doctor or consultant. The writer of this book and the publisher are not responsible for any damages or negative consequences following any of the treatments or methods highlighted in this book. Website links are for informational purposes and should not be seen as a personal endorsement; the same applies to the products detailed in this book. The reader should also be aware that although the web links included were correct at the time of writing, they may become out of date in the future.

www.ingramcontent.com/pod-product-compliance
Lightning Source LLC
Chambersburg PA
CBHW060833050426
42453CB00008B/678